B. P. Pratten

Guide Book to the Megantic, Spider, and Upper Dead River Regions

of the Province of Quebec and State of Maine

B. P. Pratten

Guide Book to the Megantic, Spider, and Upper Dead River Regions
of the Province of Quebec and State of Maine

ISBN/EAN: 9783337240752

Printed in Europe, USA, Canada, Australia, Japan

Cover: Foto ©Lupo / pixelio.de

More available books at **www.hansebooks.com**

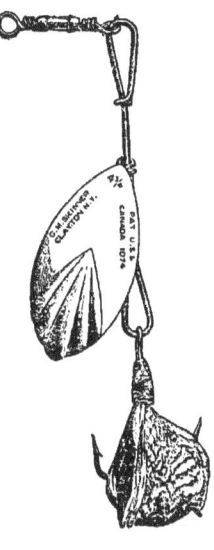

DAME, STODDARD & KENDALL,

Successors to BRADFORD & ANTHONY,

IMPORTERS AND DEALERS IN

FISHING TACKLE OF HIGH GRADE

Leonard's and Wheeler's Split Bamboo Rods.

MULTIPLYING and CLICK REELS OF EVERY DESCRIPTION

Fine Enamelled Waterproof Tapered Silk Lines.

ARTIFICIAL FLIES, FLY BOOKS, LANDING NETS.

SOLE AGENTS FOR

SKINNER'S - CELEBRATED - FLUTED - SPOON

AND NASON'S PATENT NET RING AND STAFF.

374 WASHINGTON STREET, BOSTON.

OPPOSITE BROMFIELD ST.

Guide Book to the MEGANTIC, SPIDER, and UPPER DEAD RIVER REGIONS

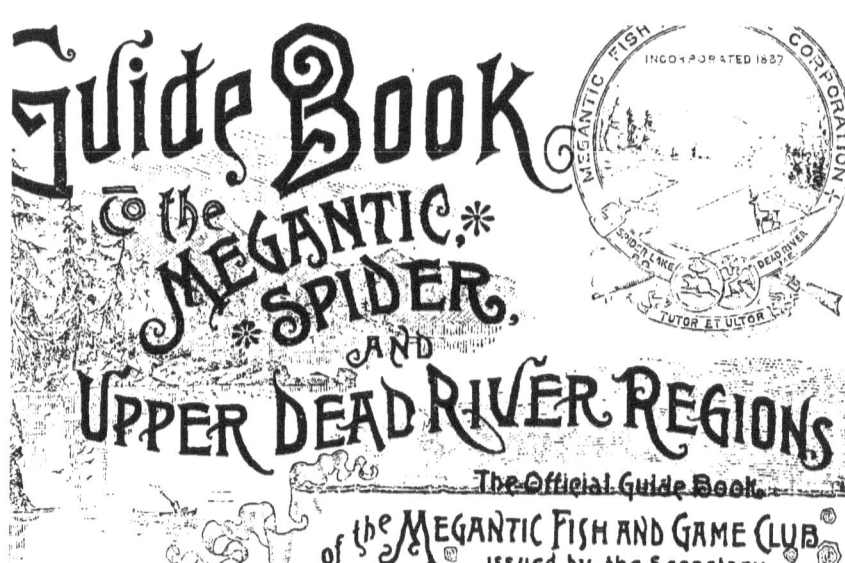

The Official Guide Book of the MEGANTIC FISH AND GAME CLUB

Issued by the Secretary

INDEX TO ADVERTISEMENTS.

The following advertisements have been selected with a view to assist members and sportsmen in general, in selecting their outfits, supplies, etc. They will be found to contain much valuable information concerning the various routes, hotels, etc.

Members will confer a favor upon the publisher by mentioning the "MEGANTIC CLUB BOOK" when corresponding with its patrons.

	PAGE		PAGE
United States Mutual Accident Association of New York	(outside)	Appleton & Litchfield, Fishing Tackle	14
		Abbey & Imbrie, Fishing Tackle	184
Dame, Stoddard & Kendall. Fishing Tackle, Cutlery, etc.	(cover) 2	United States Cartridge Co.	185
		J. S. Trowbridge & Co., Fishing Tackle	186
John P. Lovell Arms Co., Guns and Fishing Tackle	(cover) 3	A. S. Hinds, Black Fly Cream	187
		Wm. R. Schaeffer & Sons, Guns, Fishing Tackle, etc.	188
Wm. Reed & Sons, Guns and Fishing Tackle	3	J. H. Rushton, Canoes	189
Winchester Repeating Arms Co.	4	Massachusetts Arms Co., Maynard Rifles	190
Brokaw Manufacturing Co., Hunting Shirts, etc.	5	American Powder Co., "Dead Shot," "Rifle Cartridge" Powders	191
"Outing" Magazine	6		
S. Hemmenway, Tents, etc.	7	Lucke & Mitchell. Fishing Tackle, Guns, etc.	192
Canadian Pacific Railway	8	Ontario Canoe Co.	193
Steamer "Lena"	8	Thos. Jenness & Son. "Jumbolene"	194
J. Moquin, Prince of Wales Hotel	9	Strong Fire Arms Co.	195
M. J. Smith, Camp Supplies, Groceries, etc.	9	J. H. W. Huckins & Co., Canned Soups	196
Wm. H. Witt, Memphremagog House	10	Lamberson, Furman & Co., Remington Rifles, etc.	197
J. L. Coté, Sherbrooke House	11	Schoverling, Daly & Gales, Daly Three-Barrel Gun	198
Heney & Ferguson, Camping and Picnic Supplies	12	Marlin Fire Arms Co., Ballard Rifles	199
Ideal Manufacturing Co., Shot Shell Loading Sets	12	John D. & M. Williams, Roederer Champagne	200
Shipman Engine Co., Marine and Stationery Engines	13	Edward E. Clark, Boston Club Book	201

1

	PAGE		PAGE
Seavey, Foster & Bowman, "Eureka Silk"	202	Angler's Publishing Co., The "American Angler"	206
Humiston Preservation Co., "Rex Magnus"	202	Parker Bros., Guns	207
William S. Kimball & Co., Cigarettes	203	J. W. Dimick, Belcher Loader	208
E. & H. T. Anthony & Co., Photo' Outfits	203	Franklin and Megantic Railroad	208
G. W. Simmons & Co., Sportman's Goods	203	Shore Line	209
J. Stevens Arms and Tool Co., Rifles, Pistols, etc.	204	Quebec Central Railway	210
Publisher's Page	205	Central Vermont R. R.	211
N. A. Osgood, Portable Canvas Canoe	206	Maine Central R. R.	212
A. C. Gould & Co., The "Rifle"	206		

TABLE OF CONTENTS.

	PAGE		PAGE
Title	15	Moose River Region	99
Hunting and Fishing	17	Routes	101
Lake Megantic	27	Fares	115
Spider Lake	33	Guides	116
Spider River	41	Megantic Club Prospectus	119
Rush Lake	49	" " Charters	127
Arnold River and Arnold Bog	52	" " Objects	129
Trout Lake	54	" " By-Laws	136
Dead River	57	" " Rules and Regulations	141
Hathan Bog	59	" " List of Officers and Members	148
Crosby Pond	67	Quebec Game Laws	156
Arnold Pond and Chain of Ponds	71	Dominion of Canada Fishery Laws	162
Massachusetts Bog	79	Quebec Fishery Laws	164
Seven Ponds	88	Maine Fish and Game Laws	170

WILLIAM READ & SON, 107 Washington Street, Boston,
Dealers in FINE GUNS, SHOOTING & FISHING TACKLE.

SOLE BOSTON AGENTS for "W. & C. Scott & Son," Birmingham, London, and "Westley Richards," Bond St., London (Fine Hammer and Hammerless Guns.) Also Agents for "Colt," "Parker," "L. C. Smith," and all other American makes, including Rifle and Shot Double Guns, with two, also three, barrels. All the American Rifles,— "Winchester," "Bullard," "Ballard," "Wesson," "Stevens," and others; the new Winchester, '86 model, 40 calibre, 82 grains; the new Maynard, also Union Hill Ballard, Stevens' Hunter's Pet Pocket Rifle, of extraordinary accuracy and range. The new Lyman Ivory Rifle Sight. Job lot Sharp's 45 calibre Rifles, $7 each, ditto Remington, $8. Everything in line of

FISHING RODS AND TACKLE.

Split Bamboo Trout Rods, with extra tip, solid reel plate, and fine nickel-plated mountings, all in imbedded case, $10; cheaper quality ditto, $8. Lancewood Trout and Bass Rods; also, Greenheart and all others in great variety. Best hand-tied "Flies" for trout, bass, and salmon.

BAITS, LINES, HOOKS, &C., &C.

We make a specialty of fine "Field and Marine Glasses," which are made expressly for us by Lemaire, Bardon, and other noted makers in Paris, and, among others, offer a 26 ligne Military Glass at $18, also small Pocket Glass, $7, both of extra power. Cheaper grades Glasses, all prices down to $3. Also, the Sprague, Rushton, and other BOATS and CANOES. Folding Canvas Boat can be packed in a trunk. Circulars and prices sent on application.
CHAMBERLIN LOADED SHOT CARTRIDGES FOR DOUBLE GUNS. All sizes. These Cartridges are loaded with greatest accuracy, packed 25 in a box, and are very popular. Send stamps for general circular.
WILLIAM READ & SONS, 107 Washington St., Boston.

WINCHESTER · REPEATING · RIFLES.

SINGLE SHOT RIFLES,
AND REPEATING SHOT GUNS.

METALLIC
AMMUNITION,

PAPER SHELLS,
PRIMERS, &c.

The Best in the World. Send for 80 page Illustrated Catalogue.

Winchester Repeating Arms Comp'y
NEW HAVEN, CONN., U. S. A.

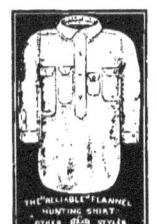 

THE "RELIABLE"
Flannel Shirts and Outing Garments.

MADE ONLY BY

BROKAW M'F'G CO.,
NEWBURGH, ... NEW YORK.

Established 1880.

ASK RETAILERS FOR THEM.

Edited by POULTNEY BIGELOW.
⊙uting
$3.00 per Annum.
Single Copies, 25 cts.

ESSENTIALLY the best GENTLEMAN'S SPORTING MAGAZINE in the world. OUTING undoubtedly affords the most interesting reading matter for every lover of the rod and gun.

THEODORE ROOSEVELT's articles on Ranch Life and Big Game Shooting (OUTING, March-August, 1886) give valuable information to those in pursuit of big game.

Fishing is an important feature in the summer numbers.

The articles on Rocky Mountain Trout, Lake George and Maine Fly Fishing, are to be found in the four midsummer months (June–September).

The International Rod and Reel Association contests of 1887, and full records, in July OUTING.

General RANDOLPH MARCY's thrilling narrative of hunting Bear, Elk, Moose, and other large game, commences in October, and will be continued in six splendidly illustrated articles.

OUTING publishes the most interesting accounts of Yachting, Canoeing, and Frontier Army Life.

An illustrated account of the memorable Coronet–Dauntless Ocean Race, by J. W. KING, Jr., U. S. N., in the June number.

Every sportsman should read the description of OUTING'S Camping Cottage (June).

Lawn Tennis, Lacrosse, Football, Cricket, Baseball, and Archery are fully treated in the columns of OUTING by specialists of each game.

Splendid illustrations and complete records.

⊙uting 140 Nassan Street, New York.

"OUTING is a periodical which deserves the heartiest welcome at the hands of busy Americans. Anything which leads them to seek outdoor life ought to be encouraged, and this OUTING does in a beguiling fashion."— *New York Tribune.*

Manufacturer of Tents of all kinds, sizes, and shapes, at low figures.

A Tent, or Common Tent, with rope ridge, used to camp out with, made any size and of best goods. Prices, from $6 to $12.

SPORTSMEN'S
Tents, Yacht & Boat Sails,
Flags and Awnings, &c.

SPECIALTIES.
Canoe Sails, all kinds.
Canoe Sail Fittings.
Canoe Sails, rigged complete with Mast, Spars, &c.
Yacht Sails and Awnings.
Steam Launch Awnings.
Cushions of all kinds.
Cork Fenders.
Sand Bags.
Life Preservers.
Cotton Duck, all widths and numbers.
Awning Goods and Fittings.
Bunting, all colors.

New Code Weather Signals.
This system of Signals has been adopted for general use by the signal Service on and after March 1, 1887. It is not complicated, and the flags can be had at $8 to $10 per set. $6 per set without Cold Wave.

Window and Store Awnings.   Canopy for Croquet Grounds, Sea Shore, Gardens, or Lawn Tennis, made in the best manner and of best goods.   Flags and Burgees of all kinds made to order.

Send Stamp for Circular and Price List.

All these goods made in the best manner and very lowest figures.
All warranted mildew and water proof at a cost of 3 cts. per yard extra.

S. HEMMENWAY, 60 South St., New York.

CANADIAN PACIFIC RAILWAY
(SHORT LINE.)
INTERNATIONAL RAILWAY COMPANY.

The direct route for Sportsmen from New York, Boston, Toronto, Montreal, and Quebec, to the best fishing and hunting grounds east of the Rocky Mountains.

Connecting with the Passumpsic, Vermont Central, Quebec Central, and Grand Trunk Railways, at Sherbrooke, P. Q., for

LAKE MEGANTIC,
  SPIDER LAKE,
    MOOSE RIVER,
      DEAD RIVER REGION,
        AND SEVEN PONDS,

landing passengers nearer these famous fish and game resorts than any other railway or stage line.

SPECIAL FAST TRAIN, for accommodation of Sportsmen, leaves Sherbrooke for Lake Megantic at 3.30 P. M. Saturdays, arriving at 6.30 P. M., and connecting with steamer "Lena" for Spider Lake.

Returning, leaves Megantic at 7.15 A. M. Mondays, arriving in Sherbrooke at 10 A. M.

New York Sportsmen purchase tickets via Connecticut River, Passumpsic, and International Railways, for Lake Megantic. From Boston, via Passumpsic and International Railways.

N. B.—Special Reduced Rates given members of the Megantic Fish and Game Club, from Sherbrooke to Spider Lake and return, including coupons on steamer, upon presentation of requisition from the Secretary.

D. E. McFEE, Supt.,
Sherbrooke, P. Q.

STEAMER "LENA,"
GEORGE FLINT, Prop'r, Three Lakes, P. Q., Canada,

Runs two trips daily between

AGNES (the village of Lake Megantic) and THREE LAKES.

TIME TABLE.

Morning Trip.—Leaves Three Lakes at 8 A. M., calling at Wooburn and Piopolis, arriving at Agnes at 9.50 A. M. Returning, leaves Agnes at 10.30 A. M., arriving at Three Lakes at 12 M.

Afternoon Trip.—Leaves Three Lakes at 2.30 P. M., arriving at Agnes at 4 P. M. Returning, leaves Agnes at 5.30 P. M.

SPECIAL ARRANGEMENTS.

The Steamer will leave Three Lakes (Mondays) at 5.30 A. M., to connect with the Canadian Pacific Railway Fast Express at 7.15 A. M. for Sherbrooke, and will also meet the same train (Saturdays) at 6.30 P. M., leaving immediately for Three Lakes upon arrival of train.

Members of the Club will be waited for until arrival of train any night, by telegraphing the proprietor at Agnes before leaving Sherbrooke. Parties telegraphing for the Steamer, and Club members, will be charged extra for the detention.

FARE, 25 CENTS EACH WAY.

Round Trip Tickets issued to Club Members at 35 cents.

PRINCE OF WALES HOTEL,

LAKE MEGANTIC, P. Q., CANADA.

THIS Hotel, situated upon the shore of Lake Megantic, near the inlet of the Chaudière River, commanding a fine view of the lake, has lately been renovated and refitted up, and is open for the accommodation of guests the year round.

Special Terms for Summer Guests and Families by the Season.

BOATS AND CARRIAGES

to let by the proprietor, at moderate charges.

Sportsmen, by notifying the proprietor, can have an express team at the station to convey baggage to the Hotel or boat; and, in the winter season (during the still-hunting), the proprietor is prepared to convey members, with their baggage, from the station to the Club headquarters and camps. Address,

J. MOQUIN, Proprietor,

Lake Megantic, P. Q.

M. J. SMITH,

FINE GROCERIES
AND PROVISIONS,

LAKE MEGANTIC, P. Q.

Keeps constantly on hand full lines of Family Groceries and Provisions, including

TEA, COFFEE, FLOUR, SUGAR, BISCUITS, &c.,

AND CANNED GOODS OF EVERY KIND.

Special Attention given to Filling Orders for Camp Supplies for Sportsmen.

Goods delivered upon the Steamer free of charge. Orders by mail will receive prompt attention, and a discount given to members of the Megantic Club.

M. J. SMITH,

Lake Megantic, P. Q., CANADA.

MEMPHREMAGOG HOUSE,

WM. H. WITT, Proprietor,

NEWPORT, - VT.

FRED A. BEEBE,.. Clerk.

SEASON OF 1887.

THE House is situated at the junction of the Connecticut and Passumpsic Rivers R.R., and the Southeastern Railway of Canada, and affords rapid and easy transit to the tourist either to the White Mountains, Boston, Portland, or New York on the south, or to Montreal, Quebec, and other points of interest on the north.

The House is large and well arranged, having all the modern conveniences, and handsomely furnished rooms for 400 guests. The hotel is situated at the head of Lake Memphremagog, and from its broad piazzas superb views of the lake, with its exquisite setting of hills and of the Green Mountains, can be enjoyed. It has been put in thorough order for the season, and has every requisite for the comfort of the transient guest, or those who want to spend the summer on the banks of the most beautiful lake in New England.

The lake is abundantly stocked with lake trout, pickerel, and other fish; and the facilities for fishing are excellent. Row boats and sail boats can always be obtained at reasonable rates. The shores of the lake furnish many romantic points for picnic parties.

A large iron steamer, the "Lady of the Lake," Capt. E. E. Cleveland, makes the tour of the lake twice a day, starting from the hotel pier. The well tilled farm and deep inlets make the shores attractive. Frequent islands diversify the scene, Province Island, through which the boundary line between the United States and Canada passes, being the largest. Owl's Head Mountain House is the first landing, a most romantic spot, with the mountain, a sheer precipice of rock, wooded at the summit, towering 2,000 feet above the lake. (Mr. GRANT ALLAN, a well-known English author, of excellent judgment, in a recent article in *Longman's Magazine*, praises highly the management of this hotel, and says that, for picturesque interest and attractive wildness, Lake George must yield the palm to Memphremagog.)

Newport, the county seat of Orleans County, is a pleasant village of 1,200 inhabitants, built on a peninsula commanding both the upper and lower portions of the lake, and with many points for far-reaching views of mountain and lake. Its air is considered by physicians to be pure and invigorating, and has been recommended by many doctors of eminence for those suffering from pulmonary affections, malaria, and hay fever.

References: NEW YORK.—FOREST H. PARKER, President Produce Exchange, 75 Front St.; WILLIAM DURYEA, 31 to 33 Park Place; C. P. DEAN, 60 Drexel Building; G. A. KISSAM, 51 Liberty St.; C. CARROL JACKSON, 21 South William St. BOSTON.—HOTEL BRUNSWICK; HOTEL VENDOME; HOTEL VICTORIA; W. RAYMOND, 296 Washington St.; 35 Milk St., Room 33; W. W. WAUGH, Manager "*Boston House Journal*," 465 Washington St., where circulars can be obtained.

TERMS: Per Day, $2, $2.50, and $3, according to location of rooms. For the Season, $8, $10.50, $14, $17.50, and $21 per week.

SHERBROOKE HOUSE,

(OPPOSITE UNION DEPOT.)

J. L. COTÊ,
Proprietor,

SHERBROOKE, P. Q., CANADA.

THE LARGEST
AND
Best Equipped Hotel
in all its appointments,
in the
EASTERN TOWNSHIPS.

Telephone Connections.

Electric Bells throughout the building.

THIS well-known and favorite house, situated in the *chef-lieu* of the Eastern Townships, is one of the oldest hotels in the country, and for nearly half a century has enjoyed a well-earned popularity that few houses can boast of. The building was destroyed by fire last winter, but has been rebuilt and refurnished, by the present proprietor, with all modern improvements and conveniences, and opened for the reception of guests this season. The dining-room, office, halls, parlors, and sleeping-rooms are large and airy,— capacity for one hundred and fifty guests. The house enjoys an enviable reputation for its well-conducted *cuisine*. On account of its convenience to the depot, its patrons save the expense of carriages, and baggage is conveyed to and from the depot without charge. The house is furnished with good billiard and pool tables, and large sample rooms. Good livery stable connected with the hotel. The town of Sherbrooke is beautifully situated upon the St. Francis and Magog Rivers, in the "Garden of the Province of Quebec," and offers special inducements to the tourist and pleasure-seeker. Special terms given to families and guests by the season.

TERMS: $2.00 PER DAY, $5.00 to $10.00 PER WEEK.

HENEY & FERGUSON,
WHOLESALE AND RETAIL DEALERS IN

CHOICE FAMILY GROCERIES,
PROVISIONS, &c.

Constantly on hand a large stock, comprising

Flour, Pork, Lard, Ham, Bacon, Butter, Cheese, Potatoes, Sugar, Tea, Coffee, Rice, Starch, Soda, Soap, Salt, Matches, Spices, Oranges, Lemons, &c.

—— ALSO ——

Canned Goods in Great Variety,
and everything required for

CAMPING OUTFITS AND PICNICS.

Special attention paid to filling orders and packing goods for safe delivery on cars or through the woods, for camping outfits and picnics.

HENEY & FERGUSON,

Wellington Street, . . SHERBROOKE, P. Q.

"IDEAL"
SHOT SHELL
Loading Set.

The only complete set that can be carried in the pocket.
Capper, De-Capper,
Rammer, Wadstarter,
Funnel, and Closer
in a neat box.

6 in. long by 2¼ x 1½, Weight, only 10 ounces. Sample by mail, $1.25. Send for Circular No. 2.

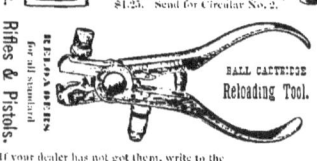

BALL CARTRIDGE
Reloading Tool.

Bullet Molds of all kinds.

If your dealer has not got them, write to the

IDEAL MFG. CO., New Haven, Conn.

THE SHIPMAN AUTOMATIC STEAM ENGINE. — Kerosene Oil Fuel.

A SUGGESTION FOR PLEASURE AND REST.

The Shipman Marine Engine is now in use in many hundred boats in nearly all parts of the world. It is built from one to five horse power. Automatic water and fuel supply. No dirt. Stationary as well as Marine. Used for pumping water, sawing wood, and operating all kinds of small machinery. Illustrated catalogue free. No skilled engineer required. **SHIPMAN ENGINE CO., 92 Pearl Street, Boston, Mass.**

Appleton & Litchfield,

Importers, Manufacturers, and Dealers in

FINE FISHING TACKLE.

OUTFITS

For Salmon, Trout, and Bass Fishing

A SPECIALTY.

LIVE HELGAMITE (DOBSON'S) FOR BASS BAIT.

304 WASHINGTON STREET,

BOSTON, MASS.

Second door north Old South Church.

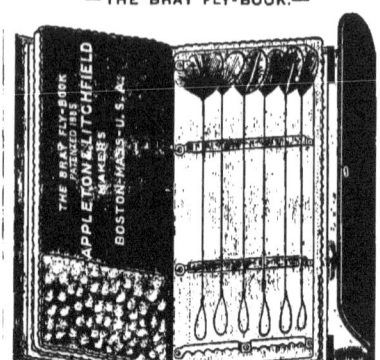

←THE BRAY FLY-BOOK.→

CAPACITY, from 2 to 12 Dozen.   PRICES, from $4.00 to $6.00.

·GUIDE BOOK·
TO THE
MEGANTIC, SPIDER, AND UPPER DEAD RIVER REGIONS
OF THE PROVINCE OF QUEBEC AND STATE OF MAINE,
INCLUDING A DESCRIPTION OF

All the Lakes and Rivers in the region, under lease to the Megantic Fish and Game Corporation, including Megantic, Spider, Rush, and Trout Lakes, the Spider and Arnold Rivers, the Chain of Ponds, Seven Ponds, Massachusetts and Arnold Bogs, and other waters in the region; also, a brief sketch of the Moose River region (recently opened up by the construction of the Canadian Pacific Railway), with a

MAP OF THE REGION,

Drawn from plans obtained from the Crown Lands Department, Quebec, other sources, and from photographs taken in the region, compiled by the Secretary for this work.

MAP SHOWING ROUTES AND RAILWAYS.
ILLUSTRATED
With engravings from photographs taken in the region by Dr. Bishop, and engraved by the Boston Engraving Company.

ALSO CONTAINS THE

PROSPECTUS, CHARTERS, BY-LAWS, RULES AND REGULATIONS, WITH LIST OF OFFICERS AND MEMBERS OF THE CLUB, THE GAME AND FISHERY LAWS OF THE PROVINCE OF QUEBEC AND STATE OF MAINE.

——— WITH FULL INFORMATION CONCERNING THE ROUTES, FARES, GUIDES, CAMPS, AND TRAILS. ———

BOSTON:
PUBLISHED BY HEBER BISHOP,
Hoffman House.
1887.

Copyright, 1887, by Heber Bishop.
All rights reserved.

HUNTING AND FISHING.

THAT the descendants of Nimrod, and the disciples of Izaak Walton, have greatly multiplied in the earth in these latter days is evident to any one who is an observer of the signs of the times. Year by year the number increases of those who devote their summer leisure to hunting and fishing, and who are on the lookout for new openings in the primeval wilderness, where they may find "fresh fields and pastures new," and where, with gun and rod, they may secure abundance of pleasure, as well as the renewal of wasted energies and a new lease of life.

The student poring over problems in books, the clergyman whose nerve force is nearly exhausted, the weary clerk, the harassed business man, the incessantly besieged editor, the professional of every grade, from the village schoolmaster to the President of the Republic,— all these and multitudes not enumerated find a solace in the midst of their labors in the prospect of a tramp through the wild woods after game, or the throwing of a fly upon waters well stocked with the finny tribes, whose cavorting has rarely been interrupted.

It is a mooted question whether the anticipation of such sport and the details of preparation, or the recounting, during the winter evenings, of one's past experiences, be the more thrilling. Next to actual participation, both prospect and retrospect are charming beyond measure. Few narratives have more of magnetic power than the stories which are told and retold of adventures in fishing and hunting, and, if they are so marvelous as to put some strain upon the credulity of the listener, the charm is greatly increased. There is always a breezy freshness to such yarns, which is captivating and exhilarating, while the imagination wanders off to make the mere recital a reality.

Whoever opens up a new vista, and introduces the lovers of sport to a fresh and desirable locality, confers an inestimable favor; for, as the advancing civilization devastates the forests and sets the rivers at work upon manufactures, the game disappears from both.

And now, if you will carefully select your fishing tackle, put in order your gun and accoutrements, pack your gripsack with necessary substantials instead of fancy goods, and come with us, we will give you something to remember for the rest of your days, where game of every kind is always plentiful, and piscatory skill can have its fullest sweep as nowhere else on this continent, east of the Rocky Mountain Range.

If Boston is a convenient point of departure, we take the evening express of the Montreal & Boston Air Line, which whirls us through a rapid succession of thriving cities and large towns, whose electric lights make the first few hours seem like a moving panorama of Fairy Land, with rapid alternations of light and shade, glimpses of gleaming waters, and peeps at pleasant villas, into the dark shadows of mountain gorges, and out across verdant lawns sleeping in the moonlight, all combining to make an ever-changing kaleidoscope of beauty, most weird and enchanting.

At Wells River Junction, other Pullmans from New York, via New Haven and Connecticut River, are joined to our train; and then over the Passumpsic Railroad through the White Mountain region, whose famous peaks loom up in strangely solemn grandeur by night, we rush toward Canada with the alacrity of an American "boodler," or a defaulting cashier. The morning finds us at Newport, and skirting the shores of the beautiful Lake Memphremagog and the smaller Massawippi, threading our way down the interesting valley of the river of the same name to Sherbrooke, in the Province of Quebec. At the latter place, we have an opportunity to stop over a few hours, and in the afternoon change to the Canadian Pacific Railroad, and, taking an easterly course, we reach Lake Megantic village. A delightful sail across this picturesque lake to Three Lakes, with a tramp of half a mile,

Steaming up Spider Lake.

brings us to the wharf on Spider Lake; and nine o'clock in the evening finds us landing from a natty steamer at the new and elegant Club House of

THE MEGANTIC FISH AND GAME CORPORATION,

where a good supper, pleasant rooms, and comfortable beds are awaiting us, and make us glad that it is to be our home for a few days. A chat upon the spacious piazzas, a dreamy study of Spider Lake lying in its *robe de nuit* before us, mutual congratulations upon the assurance that we have at last found "just the right place," the reeling off of the latest yarn about the sport hereabouts, and each one

. . . " wraps the drapery of his couch
About him, and lies down to pleasant dreams."

Doubtless, no one of our party would feel at all complimented on being called the successor of Benedict Arnold ; yet he was among the earliest of notable tramps to explore this region, when, in 1775, he was sent by General Schuyler on an expedition into Canada, through the eastern wilderness, by way of the Kennebec and Dead River regions, a most interesting account of which will be found in Spark's History. Starting from Cambridge, Mass., on September 18, with eleven hundred men, and taking transports at Newburyport for the Kennebec River, he passed through a series of hardships which make a thrilling record. "Eleven hundred men with arms, ammunition, and all the apparatus of war, burdened with clothing to protect them against the inclemency of the weather, were to pass through a region uninhabited, wild and desolate, forcing their bateaux against swift currents, and carrying them and their contents on their own shoulders around rapids and cataracts, over craggy precipices, and through

MASSAWIPPI LAKE.

morasses, till they should reach the French settlements in Canada, a distance of more than two hundred miles."

Throughout the entire route, they encountered the most discouraging disasters and exciting episodes, and were until November 13 in reaching Point Levis, opposite Quebec. Aaron Burr, then a young man and afterward Vice-President of the United States, accompanied Arnold on this expedition. Their route lay through this region, and near us is the site of one of their camps, from which an occasional memento is obtained. One of their old bayonets, half eaten up by more than a century of rust, is in possession of the Secretary of the Megantic Fish and Game Club.

Possibly, some of our party cannot stop to enjoy the pleasures described further on in this book, but would like to make a hurried trip to the celebrated Rangeley Lakes, thirty or forty miles to the eastward, and return to the exigencies of business. If so, from the Spider Lake to the Seven Ponds, thence *via* Tim Pond to Eustis, Me.; from the latter place by stage-coach and narrow guage railroad, along the picturesque valley of the Androscoggin River, *via* Kingfield and the Rangeleys. Through all the trip, every mile presents points of special and romantic interest. From here, the homeward route lies through Farmington, Me., the prettiest country town in the State, where one finds strong temptation to stay awhile. Here we connect with the Maine Central Railroad, running through lovely landscapes and charmingly quiet pastoral scenes to Portland, where the lover of nature ought to spend at least a day or two among the hundreds of islands in Casco Bay, rivaling in interest the famous Thousand Islands of the Upper St. Lawrence. From Portland, one can take his choice of routes to Boston, going by either division of the Boston & Maine,— the western, *via* Berwick, Haverhill, and Lawrence, or the eastern, which follows the sea coast; or an excellent line of steamers will afford a pleasant ocean trip, which is full of interest.

After such an outing comes the tug of war! It *is* a hard thing, after the freedom of wilderness life, to settle down and take up the cross of daily toil; to put away the roundabouts and corduroys where moth doth not corrupt; to put the trusty gun on the brackets, and stand the fishing rod in its sheath in the corner of a dark closet; to lay aside the flannel shirt, redolent with the aroma of oil of tar and pennyroyal, and feel once more the tyranny of the linen collar; to doff the free-and-easy suit, and frame one's self in "store clothes"; to exchange the flavor of game for the odor of rumpsteaks and baked beans, and the pure mountain air for the stifling atmosphere of the counting-room, the laboratory, or the study, while one bows meekly (perhaps?) to the tyranny of fashion and the conventional exactions of etiquette.

And yet, through all this gleams the bright recollection of "when we were in the woods," with voluminous stories of exciting adventures at Spider Lake and Megantic, Seven Ponds, *et al*, when old comrades meet to "fight their battles o'er again," and plan the next campaign. Verily, the enjoyment of such evenings in "the afterward" is worth the full cost of the trip; and it is no wonder that the participants grow infatuated, until, in the exuberance of their enthusiasm, they are unconsciously carried beyond the severe limits of exact statement, and lean a little toward exaggerated hyperbole!

The man is to be pitied who has no taste for roving in the woods, and can talk of nothing but the dry practicalities of his business, or of the still more unattractive technicalities of a profession; who does not know a trout from a mackerel except by the stripes on the latter, or would look for a black bass to take a "squid," or take along a rod and reel if invited to go blue-fishing.

There is a wholesome discipline as well as recuperation in a few weeks of camp life, which rounds out the character of a man, freeing him from many a foolish notion and fitting him for greater usefulness in his calling. The perceptive faculties are quickened, the mind broadened; it lifts one out of the ruts of daily life, renews his vigor, cheers and purifies his spirit and oils the creaking mental machinery so that he can accomplish more than before, with much less strain.

Moose Head.— Shot in Spider River October, 1886.

The clergyman preaches better and shorter sermons, and uses fresh metaphors and similes, while the flock think less about a change of shepherd. The business man finds that, after all, the world has jogged along about as usual, and that the fresh grip he can take upon his affairs more than compensates for the loss of a few possible bargains or turns he has missed in the market. The lawyer sees points more clearly, the physician grows more skillful, the statesman becomes less a demagogue, and more a man of the people, the journalist's articles grow crisp, the pedagogue learns to mingle more of common sense with his "book larnin'," and all the dusty highways and byways in the routine of daily life everywhere are made smoother and pleasanter by such out-door experiences.

But, while we have been moralizing, we had nigh

forgotten that we were to act as chaperon to the party who for the first time visit the territory leased by the Megantic Association, and will proceed with the main purpose of this work, and give a brief but practical description of the different lakes, streams, and forests that offer so many attractions to all lovers of good hunting and fishing.

Seven Pound Trout, caught in Spider River June, 1886.

LAKE MEGANTIC.

LAKE MEGANTIC.

This lake is the largest in the whole territory, being twelve miles long by one to four miles wide, and contains over forty miles of shore line. It is fed by the Lower Spider River, which empties Spider and Rush Lakes, and the Arnold River; the river enters the lake a few rods from Flint's Mills. It also receives the waters of the Annance River, which enters near Wooburn Wharf, the Victoria River in Victoria Bay, the Sandy River at Echo Bay, and numerous other small streams. At its outlet, the Chaudière River takes its origin from Chaudière Bay, upon which the village of Agnes, Lake Megantic, is situated.

The village contains two churches, a dozen or more stores, six hotels, two steam sawmills, and about two hundred inhabitants. It is the present terminus of the International Railway, or Short Line, a connecting link of the Canadian Pacific Railway, although the rails are laid twenty miles beyond, across the international boundary. The village is very prettily situated upon the lake shore and both sides of the river, the principal industry of the inhabitants being lumbering. The railway is built out two hundred feet, upon a large and capacious wharf, to facilitate the handling of lumber; and the steamer "Lena," owned by Mr. George Flint, of Three Lakes, calls at this wharf upon all trips.

Sportsmen will find the Prince of Wales Hotel, Mr. Moquin, proprietor (which is only a step from the wharf, and between it and the depot), a clean, neat, well-kept house, with a genial and obliging host.

The trip on the steamer from Agnes to Three Lakes, which is situated at the head of the lake, occupies about an hour, the distance ten miles.

The scenery along the route is very romantic and variegated, the different ranges of hills and mountains presenting a changed appearance at each half-mile of the journey. At Rocky Point is the pretty summer residence of W. B. Ives, Esq., the member for Richmond and Wolfe, and Mr. Rufus H. Pope, of Cookshire, while opposite and a little higher up is the summer house of Mr. T. C. Jones, of Winnipeg, Man. The "Hermit's Den," containing a genuine hermit, is at Sandy Point. After reaching the latter point, the Boundary Mountains come into view, showing the Scotch Cap, Saddleback, Gosford, Boil, Snow, and other mountains, giving a most charming landscape view upon a clear day. One cannot help comparing the scene, and the invigoration that is already perceptible throughout the system, from being in an atmosphere three thousand feet above sea level; with the depression, heat, smoke, and dust of Boston and New York Cities,— besides, an appetite, which is the first legitimate result of invigoration, is engendered at once by the trip across the lake. And who of the parties that have visited the lake can deny that upon reaching Three Lakes they had an appetite that would do justice to an Esquimau?

The shores, particularly the eastern side, are dotted here and there with the farms of the settlers. Wild fowl can be seen at every trip, affording ample opportunity for testing firearms from the deck of the steamer.

The village of Three Lakes is situated at the head of the lake, upon a neck of land cornering upon Megantic, Spider, and Rush Lakes; hence its name. Six years ago, an Indian camp was the only landmark; and it is due entirely to the energy and perseverance of one man that a village, containing a steam mill, hotel, store, post-office, schoolhouse, and half a dozen dwelling-houses, has been established. The name of Mr. George Flint will always be associated with Three Lakes. This gentleman, after choosing the present site for his steam mill, built a steam launch, and placed it upon the lake, established a post-office, now having a daily mail, opened up a road connecting with the village of Megantic, built a road across to Spider Lake (half a mile distant), and thus laid the foundation for a thriving little village.

Mr. William E. Latty, the fish and game overseer of the Club, owns the hotel; and members of the Club, and sportsmen in general, will always find good accommodations at his house, and an excellent table.

The lake has numerous bays,— Victoria, Sandy, Moose, and Chaudière Bays. The illustration (page 26) is from a photograph taken from the upper gallery of the Prince of Wales Hotel, looking west, with the Megantic Mountains in the distance. The finest view upon the lake is from the hill leading down to Sandy Bay, looking south, taking in the Boundary and other mountains in Maine. All the streams emptying into the lake abound with brook trout. The Victoria River affords good trout fishing, and is navigable with small boats for quite a distance. This river takes its origin in the township of Clinton, and, flowing through the township of Marston, empties into Megantic. The Annance River empties in at the head of the lake, near the Wooburn Wharf. It is a small stream; but the lower two miles are navigable with small boats, the water being still and quite deep in places. The shores of this portion are favorite feeding grounds for deer and moose,

JOE MARIE, Indian Guide, Megantic

and many are shot here every season by "jacking." Very good fishing can be had in the stream, the trout averaging small; but it is a favorite fishing ground on account of its being easy of access.

Near the mouth of the Annance River is Annance Bog, a small body of dead water, extending back nearly a mile in a southerly direction from the lake. This bog is a very favorite resort for deer, moose, and caribou, as it affords excellent feeding grounds; and during the month of September it gives good sport to those fond of jacking, which heretofore has been about the only method of shooting about these bogs. It is not at all uncommon to see five or six deer in one evening's jacking in this bog, the adjoining river, and Rush Lake.

The fishing in Lake Megantic, as in all other large lakes, is very uncertain. The lake is full of fine lake trout, weighing as high as twenty-five pounds, as is shown by the poachers' night lines, nets, etc., which have been used with impunity in the lake up to a recent date. In Chaudière Bay, Moose Bay, and at the various inlets, speckled trout will rise to a fly; but the months of June and September are the only months in which the lake trout will take a bait in legitimate fishing, except at the outlet of the lake (Chaudière River), where there is excellent fishing, speckled trout rising readily to the fly all through the season. Some very fine "strings of trout" have been taken by casting from the bridge across the Chaudière River, at the outlet of Lake Megantic; but of late years, since the village has sprung up and increased in population, the fishing, as a natural consequence, has deteriorated. Good fishing can be had by going down the Chaudière River, which is navigable by small boats, although the current is pretty swift. Sportsmen fond of trolling or bait-fishing for lake trout will find Rocky Point and vicinity the best grounds for the purpose. Hall's Point, which forms one of the sides of Chaudière Bay, is a favorite trolling ground. Trout can be caught through the ice, at the head of Lake Megantic, at any time in the winter, the open season for lake trout commencing on December 15. Last winter, a trout was caught through the ice in this locality, weighing twenty-one pounds.

SPIDER LAKE FROM THE CARRY. (Autumn)

SPIDER LAKE.

SPIDER LAKE has been aptly named "the Geneva of Canada." Surrounded upon all sides by lofty ranges of mountains, and lying in an elevated atmosphere three thousand feet above sea level, it is one of the prettiest inland lakes in Canada, and a more delightful spot for seeking relaxation and seclusion in the summer time cannot be found. Next to Megantic, it is the largest body of water in the region, being between three and four miles long, and from half a mile to three miles wide, and is about thirty-five feet higher than Lake Megantic, from which it is separated by a carry of less than three-quarters of a mile. The proper name of the lake is "Macannamac," the old Indian name, and as such it is written on all the maps; and it seems a pity that its original name should become so rapidly obsolete. The name signifies "Father, or Source of the Waters," as it is the first body of water across the watershed on the Canadian side of the boundary, and the headwater of the Chaudière River. The common name "Spider" has been given the lake from its supposed resemblance in form to the insect of that name, being composed of a large central body of water, with numerous deep bays or inlets indenting the shores, and, although much smaller in size than its neighbor Megantic, it is said to contain more miles of shore. The lake is only a couple of miles north of the Maine border, and three-quarters of a mile from Megantic. It is by far the prettiest sheet of water in the Club region, and on this account, besides its many facilities, it has been chosen upon as the site of the Club House and headquarters of the Club.

The lake is fed by the Upper Spider River, the Indian River, and several small brooklets, and is emptied into Rush Lake and Megantic by the Rapid and Lower Spider Rivers. It is three miles from Lake Megantic by water through Rush Lake, which is not navigable for the first three-quarters of a mile, by reason of the rapids between Spider and Rush Lakes.

The Club House will be located on the southern shore, commanding a fine view of the Boundary Mountains in the east, and other chains. The northern shore of the lake is partially settled; but upon the southern shore there is not a settler, and all the land on this side is leased to the Club. About a mile and a half from the carry, at the foot of the lake, is a very pretty island, containing about fifteen acres of land,—" McMinn's Island,"—in honor of Major William McMinn, a recluse major in the Confederate Army, who has a cabin upon its shore; and behind this island, upon its southern shore, no better black-bass fishing can be found anywhere in the lake. An old fallen pine lies upon the shore, projecting out in ten or fifteen feet of water, and from under its branches the writer has allured many a black bass, ranging from three to eight pounds in weight. They will rise to a fly in July, and take a live bait all through the season. Immediately opposite this island is a low sandy beach, with an occasional reed and water lily growing here and there; and, almost any time during the warm weather, deer can be seen coming out to escape the flies and to drink, and particularly toward sunset, when

> The dying day
> Is slowly fading in the purple west,
> And Nature dons her sable robes for rest.
> The Sun, from gorgeous chariot whose glow

TAXIDERMIST'S CAMP. (Spicer Lake.)

Lights into weird radiance all above, below,
Smiles farewell glances to the Evening Star,
Peeping coquettish from blue depths afar,—
And takes his way.

Just above the island, on the same shore, is Thomas' Point, an elevated bit of land sloping down to

Along the Sand Beach (Bishop's Cove).

a rocky shore, which has been partially cleared off, and a log cabin erected. It commands a fine view of the entire lake, and is the shooting lodge of Mr. D. Thomas, Registrar of Sherbrooke, one of the pioneers of Spider Lake.

A little higher up the lake, and around Thomas' Point, is Bishop's Cove, a shallow bay covered with reeds, and containing a beautiful sand beach. The water in summer, for a distance of fifteen or twenty rods from the beach, is not over a foot or

WHITE BIRCH CAMP. (From a Photograph.)

eighteen inches deep; and this cove is the favorite place for deer to come out, while behind it is a natural deer park. During the months of June, July, and August, deer come out every day; and many times has the writer watched them for hours, and admired their graceful movements as they frolicked upon the beach.

A little way above this cove, midway between it and the Spider River, is "White Birch Camp," the summer house of Dr. Bishop, which is very prettily situated among a clump of white birch and poplar trees, upon a bluff overlooking the lake.

There is good bass fishing with troll or fly all along this shore, at the head of the lake, and on the opposite shore, in front of the different points. The Spider River empties into the lake, in the southeast corner, over a low, sandy, shallow marsh, with scarcely enough water to float a boat; but, as soon as the river is reached, the waters deepen quickly. The Indian River empties in on the northern shore, opposite White Birch Camp. It is navigable for a short distance up, and one can get fair trout fishing near its outlet. Many deer have been killed upon its banks by jacking, which is the universal method of hunting them in this section. There is also good jacking in nearly all the bays in Spider Lake in the early autumn. Occasionally, one can get a shot at a deer in daytime, swimming in the lake or feeding upon the banks. The method of "still-hunting" them with canoes is as follows: The guide takes the stern of the canoe with the paddle, while the party who is to do the shooting sits in the bow with the rifle. As soon as the deer comes out, the guide turns the canoe straight facing him, and glides along noiselessly as long as the deer is drinking or feeding. As soon as he raises his head, the guide stops, remaining in a cataleptic condition; for the deer will allow a canoe to be paddled up within ten yards, so long as he sees no motion, provided the wind is favorable, and he does not "get on the scent." The moment the deer

AN INTERIOR, WHITE BIRCH CAMP.

resumes feeding, the guide will put in and paddle until he again looks up, and so on until the canoe is within range, and the report of the rifle is the first warning taken of danger. Often, though, as the canoe approaches, the deer will become wary and uneasy, and the first thing noticed will be a shake of his tail; the next moment, as he lifts and arches his head and neck, the tail goes up perpendicularly, and away goes the deer through the water and into the woods like an arrow. A quick aim and pull of the trigger must be made the instant the tail begins to move, accompanied by arching of the neck, as it is considered by the most inveterate huntsmen as an infallible sign that the deer anticipates danger, and will not remain another moment. This method of deer hunting is one of the most enjoyable. There is much depending upon the skill of the guide, as well as controlling yourself when the deer is watching you, and you are only waiting for him to lower his head once more to give the guide an opportunity to send you within range. Less than a mile from Spider Lake, and situated between the North Bay and Lake Megantic, is

EGG POND,

a small body of water less than half a mile long. It is nearly round in shape, as its name signifies, and at one time contained innumerable trout. On account of its proximity to settlers, it has been pretty well depleted, very probably by the use of nets. The variety of trout contained in it is very fine, and when one is caught it is a large one. With protection and restocking, it could again be made a good fish pond. On account of its proximity to Spider Lake, it is well worth a visit and trial.

SPIDER LAKE. (Looking east from Thomas' Point.)

"BIG BOG." (Off the Upper Spider River.)

THE SPIDER RIVER.

 T is almost impossible to do justice to the Spider River in writing a description of it for a guide book, which should be terse and practical. A more charming stream for the lover of nature, and true sportsman, cannot be found, with its abundance of attractions.

Arising among the Boundary Mountains in the extreme limit of the Canadian territory, it is made up of several small rivulets, which, after congregating together, form two main branches,— the east and most important branch taking up the ramifications in the township of Louise, the west draining the more distant portion of the township of Ditchfield. The two tributaries join at a point five miles from the lake.

The east branch flows through what is called the "brûlé" or burnt land, a large tract of about six thousand acres that has been completely burnt over and destroyed by forest fires. From the forks and for a distance of a mile below, the river is not navigable, but the lower four miles are comparatively dead water, and navigable all the way to Spider Lake.

The river has the reputation of being a most prolific trout stream, and despite the steady and almost unlimited drain made upon it the last ten years, prior to the Club's acquiring the lease of it, it still affords excellent fishing, and with moderate protection and restocking can again be made one of the finest trout streams in the province. That portion flowing through the "brûlé" is rapid, with the exception of a few pools and stretches of dead water. It also contains two or three small ponds, dilatations of the stream,

SCENE ON WHARF AT WHITE BIRCH CAMP. (Spider Lake.)

which afford excellent sport; they are situated nearly three miles above the forks. The fishing all the way down the stream from the ponds to the forks is very good, the trout at present running small. From the forks to the "landing," which is at the head of navigation, the fish run a little larger, and pounders are not unfrequently taken, while, in the mouth of June, as large as three or four pound trout are taken. From the landing to the lake, about four miles, the river is still very winding and with deep pools. Last season, a trout was caught here weighing seven pounds. It is this portion that offers so many inducements to the canoeist. Upon each bank is a fringe of lily-pads, with a bordering of tall grass and hardhack bushes, with the green trees and mountains in the background. Game of all kind is seen in paddling up the stream. Deer come out to drink, and feed upon the water lilies; wild ducks, blue herons, or kingfishers are startled at every turn and bend in the river.

A fortnight ago, the writer, in paddling up the river a distance of two miles, came upon five deer feeding along the banks, which shows the excellent results from the endeavors of our indefatigable game wardens. Deer-jacking has been the invariable procedure upon this river both in and out of season until the present season, when the game laws were commenced to be enforced by paid wardens, and the results have been very encouraging. There is no better place upon the whole preserve for deer than the Upper Spider River, the whole of its navigable distance. There are innumerable bogs leading out of the river, and they afford excellent feeding grounds. Some of these bogs are half a mile long, and a boat can be floated through them. The most prolific of them is the Big Bog, which is situated upon the northern shore, a couple of miles from the lake. Many deer and moose are killed in this bog yearly, it being at the terminus of several "runways" extending back into the woods, and is the favorite spot for jack-hunting. The method of jacking deer and moose is as follows: A lamp with reflector is placed upon a stick or support in the bow of the canoe, so arranged that all the light is thrown directly forward, and all rays excluded from reaching the boat and its occupants. The guide takes the stern with the paddle, the one who is to do the shooting being seated in the bow, behind the jack, rifle in hand. The utmost quiet is enjoined by the guide, who propels the canoe along noiselessly, without removing his paddle from the water, turning the canoe at his will, so as to scan each bank. It is hard to say from what standpoint the deer views the jack-light. Some claim that the deer imagines it to be the moon with its reflection upon the water, its close proximity not being suspected; while others say that the deer notices something unusual in the light, but regards it with curiosity, and not seeing any objects about it, or hearing any noise to alarm it, stands stock-still until shot. Whatever are the deer's thoughts, if the wind does not give him the scent, he will stand, in many cases, till the light is within ten feet, and not exhibit the slightest alarm. The deer is generally heard in the water before seen, the sound bringing one's heart into the mouth, and setting the canoe vibrating from the rapid pulsations; the guide quietly turns the light in the direction of the sound, and glides the canoe steadily along toward the spot from whence the sound proceeded. The first thing noticeable is what appears like two small balls of fire in the darkness, the reflection of the light upon the deer's eyes. Slowly and steadily the boat is pushed on, the moments seeming like hours to the expectant hunter, till gradually the form of the deer becomes outlined, and the animal looms up nearer and nearer. If the hunter is new at the business, the guide generally gives the signal when to fire, and the animal is dropped.

From reading the above, one would imagine that it was easy to kill a deer by jack-hunting; but such is not always the case. Almost invariably a sportsman will miss the first deer he fires at in the night, and subsequent ones till he becomes more composed, and takes a more careful aim. Much also depends upon

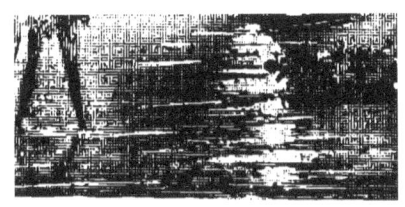

HUNTING MOOSE BY "JACK-LIGHT." (Spider River.)

...ose will at once inform the deer of danger, and he will disappear before the guide, as the slightest ...st breath of wind wafted toward the deer will warn him of danger; or, if being plainly seen. The lea... so as to swing or sway the lantern, the deer will become alarmed, and the boat becomes unsteady... ng like a warhorse.

disappear snorting and blow... do not stand so quietly at an approaching jack, and then they are hunted Late in the season, dee... being attached to it in such a manner that the lantern can be quickly with a dark lantern, a str... soon as the boat is within range. This method is the common one for and noiselessly opened as ...ile, are not so hard to get up to as deer, if a dark lantern is used. The jacking moose, which, as ...otice anything, but will keep on eating or walking about till fired upon; but, moose does not appear to ...cretionary to retire with the canoe as quickly as possible, as they will often if wounded, it is always ...it, recognizing in it an enemy, and many instances are recorded in which a come straight for the lig...lace in jacking moose at close quarters. Although not considered a very sharp contest has taken ...ng deer, and one which is prohibited by statute law in certain localities, there sportsmanlike way of shoc... that is very fascinating to one accustomed to the practice, so that often one is a pleasure attached to it...uty of venison in the larder, and with no intention of shooting a deer, but will go out jacking with ...cess and watch the deer, seeing how near one can get to them. The writer merely to go through the '...er, while jacking, near enough to touch it with the muzzle of the rifle. has been paddled up to a '...lness in a calm evening while jacking up the river, that is very impressive.

There is a solemn s' ...broken by some bird flying over the canoe, or a muskrat quietly swimming Occasionally the stillness ...light, and suddenly dives under the water, making a splash that, if taken across the stream sees ... you, and nearly upset the canoe. But, if no game is stirring about, nothing unawares, is sure to sta...

WINTER CAMP ON THE SPIDER RIVER.

is heard but the faint ripple of the water against the bark upon the bow of the canoe, and one often imagines the boat at a standstill, and the shores receding down stream, where

> Long shadows sweep
> Across the shimmering streams and leafy bogs,
> And silence reigns, save where the piping frogs
> Hold carnival amid the deepening shade,
> Vociferous in evening serenade;
> Or solemn owl — as maidens sometimes do —
> Chants nightly a monotonous, "To who!"
> With pathos deep.

RUSH LAKE.

DILATATION of the Lower Spider River, with a bordering marsh or bog, forms Rush Lake, so named from the reeds and rushes growing all over it. It is quite a large body of water in the springtime, covering an area of a mile in length, and from a quarter to a half mile in breadth. It is fed by the Rapid Spider River, which empties Spider Lake some three-quarters of a mile distant, and by a couple of other small streams. It is situated about a mile from Lake Megantic, and is emptied by the Lower Spider River, which, after being joined by the Arnold River a few rods from the outlet of Rush Lake, flows into Lake Megantic.

During the summer months, particularly in a dry season, the entire lake, except the channel, is boggy, all the water thickly covered with lily-pads, interspersed with tall reeds and rushes, the banks containing alder bushes, while here and there are arms and inlets forming bogs, some nearly a mile long, through which a boat can be pushed. It is in these bogs that so many deer and moose have been shot by jack-hunting during the early autumn, as they become valuable feeding grounds during the period between sunset and the early morning. One can often see a deer or moose in the afternoon or evening in these bogs, by paddling up the lake.

Duck shooting in Rush Lake is very fine during the migratory period, in the fall. Immense flocks of ducks frequent the lake, and rendezvous there overnight. The best time for the duck shooting is after the middle of October, and up to the time the ice begins to form.

Camping at Rush Lake (Foster's Clearing).

Fishing in the lake does not amount to much, owing to the inability to cast a fly on account of the rushes; but at the inlet at the foot of the rapids is excellent trout fishing in the mouth of June, while all through the winter trout can be caught through the ice at the head of the lake. There is very good black-bass fishing at the foot of Rush Lake, particularly where the Arnold River joins the Spider. Bass will take the fly (Polka, Blue Bass, Silver Doctor, or Full-winged Ibis being the favorite flies) in July, and minnows (live bait) at any time in the season. Minnows can be caught anywhere in the lake with a landing net and a few crumbs of bread. A small trout stream enters one of the bogs at the upper right hand corner of the lake, which is accessible with a boat, unless a particularly dry season; and in this stream a mess of trout can be taken at any time by casting from the boat. Upon the left hand shore, just before entering the lake, is a small clearing,— "Foster's Clearing,"— so named from Andrew Jackson Foster, one of the pioneer guides in the region, who lost his life crossing Lake Megantic on the early fall ice. He was returning from the Chaudière River, where he had been for camp supplies, and had a bag of flour upon his back; the ice broke, and the weight upon his neck drove him through the hole, from which he never escaped. A mound of earth a few steps from the bank marks the spot where it is said his bones lie. The illustration on the opposite page is from a photograph taken in the edge of Foster's Clearing, and is the spot where the writer and Mr. Woodruff, of New York, Vice-President of the Club, pitched their first tent in the Megantic region, and shot their first buck.

There is a trail leading from the dam on Spider Lake to the head of Rush Lake; and the "Whisky Trail," named from the purposes for which it was originally used, starts in at this place, and extends to the Chain of Ponds, crossing the international boundary between Arnold and Crosby Ponds. This trail has been in existence over twenty years, and was extensively patronized by whisky smugglers and "bounty jumpers" during the war. Rush Lake is easily accessible from Megantic by small boats, but not from Spider Lake, by reason of the rapids between the two lakes.

THE ARNOLD RIVER AND ARNOLD BOG.

HE Arnold River takes its most southern origin in the township of Wooburn, among the mountains forming what is called the "Ox-Bow," the Boundary range of mountains curving along the watershed of the Arnold River upon one side, and the Cupsuptic and Magalloway on the other. Another branch (the west branch) takes its origin in Chesham, near Saddleback and the Megantic Mountains, the Megantics forming the watershed between the Arnold (west branch) and the Salmon Rivers, both in the Province of Quebec. After following a very winding course, estimated at forty or fifty miles, the Arnold River empties into the Spider just at the outlet of Rush Lake, a mile from Lake Megantic. The water of the Arnold River is very clear and cold, and the trout excellent. The river is navigable for fifteen miles (to the head of the meadows) from Lake Megantic. There is good fishing along the meadows (about five miles long), but the best fishing is in the rapid waters above the Wooburn Bridge.

ARNOLD BOG

is situated at the headwaters of the river. It begins near the boundary, extending northward, and is about five miles long. It is low and marshy, very much like Massachusetts Bog, but wider, and contains more water. Upon the west shore is the Boundary range of mountains, looking very much like the mountains upon the west side of Massachusetts Bog.

The bog is full of trout, and it is said to contain land-locked salmon as well, the small fry that were put into Lake Megantic four or five years ago having found their way up the Arnold River, from the lake, to the bog.

A nice camp is built upon the east side of the bog near the outlet, the property of Mr. John Danforth, of Camp Caribou, Lake Parmachenee, the camp having been built and furnished before the territory was leased to the Club by the Quebec Government.

The Club will put some boats in the coming season, and cut a trail through from Wooburn. There is already a trail leading from the bog southward along the Magalloway River to Parmachenee Lake.

This bog is the home of the caribou and moose, and offers the best grounds for hunting large game. Still-hunters in the fall of the year will find Arnold Bog a veritable sportsman's Paradise. The bog is about fifteen miles south of Wooburn village, and ten miles west of the Seven Ponds, and about twelve miles north of Parmachenee Lake. It is very rarely visited from the Canadian side of the boundary, although on Canadian territory.

TROUT LAKE.

TROUT LAKE is about five miles, in an easterly direction, from the head of Lake Megantic, and is situated in the township of Clinton, near the town line of Marston. There is no direct trail cut from Megantic; and the lake is usually reached by crossing Lake Megantic from Three Lakes, and driving back upon the government road about three miles from Mr. Ryan's residence upon Megantic to the farm of Mr. Cusineau, a French settler, from whose place a tramp of two miles will cover the distance to the lake. The route is very hilly, but affords an excellent view of the surrounding country, the scenery alone being worth the tramp in. The lake is situated at the base of a very steep hill, over which the trail passes, is in shape and size very much like L Pond, of the Seven Ponds group, with as good a reputation for trout fishing. The lake empties by a circuitous little stream into the Annance River. It is the best pond for trout upon the Canadian side of the boundary, trout rising to the fly from May till October, and averaging half a pound in weight, with an occasional one up to as high as four pounds. The four trout in the initial of this chapter were caught in this lake, and weighed nine pounds, the largest one weighing over three pounds.

There is a good camp and lean-to at Trout Lake, and a boat will be placed upon the lake the coming season, and possibly a more direct trail cut from Lake Megantic. Deer often come out upon its shores, and are quite plentiful in the vicinity.

LEAN-TO AT HATHAN BOG. (Dead River)

DEAD RIVER.

THE nearest water from Spider Lake, after crossing the international boundary into Maine, is the extreme headwaters of the Dead River, one of its branches arising just over the watershed, and is a small creek that can be stepped across till it reaches the Upper Hathan Bog, which empties into the lower bog after a distance of nearly a mile between the two. Crosby Pond, which is near by, and Cranberry Bog, from another branch, meeting the other waters in the Lower Hathan Bog, which flows in a southeasterly direction till it joins with the Gore Stream just below Horseshoe Pond. The Gore Stream has its origin in Big Northwest Pond (one of the Seven Ponds group), and flows northerly through Massachusetts Bog to Arnold Pond, thence easterly through Mud and Horseshoe till it joins the Hathan Bog waters. From here, the river flows in a southerly direction through the Chain of Ponds proper, including Round, Long, Beaver, Bag, and Lower Ponds. From this point, the river flows south and east till it empties into the Kennebec River.

HATHAN BOG (upper portion).

HATHAN BOG.

A LOW, marshy body of water situated a mile from the boundary, and five miles from Spider Lake, is called Hathan Bog, from an old lumberman of that name who first cut the lordly pines that make this region famous, and floated them down the Dead River into the Kennebec. It is divided into two separate portions, the upper and lower bog, with nearly a mile of stream intervening. The broad expanse at the head of the upper bog, shown in the illustration opposite, is erroneously put down as Beaver Pond on some of the maps. This portion is very shallow, not over a foot deep in dry weather, with a very muddy bottom, which grows an endless variety of aquatic plants, and is covered with lily-pads, etc. It was originally formed by beavers damming the stream a few rods below. There are no less than three beaver dams in this portion, over two of which boats have to be drawn, unless the water is very high.

After leaving the open space, the bog narrows to a creek, navigable all the way for over a mile to the foot of the bog, where there is now constructed a dam for driving logs.

The stream emptying this portion runs through a rocky almost inaccessible place for three-quarters of a mile, till it reaches the Lower Hathan Bog, which is much smaller than the upper one, and about half a mile long; it is more properly a creek. The stream emptying Crosby Pond enters here a few rods from the head of the bog. The remains of an old dam lie at the foot of this portion, and from here the Dead River proper commences, forming the branch which joins the stream emptying the other ponds on the Coburn Gore, at the forks between Horseshoe and Round Ponds. The land about both bogs has been completely burnt over, and is fast being covered with small second-growth shrubbery, while less than a mile distant, on all sides, are the Boundary Mountains, with their green verdure and heavy timber.

Beaver constructing Dam

Hathan Bog, considering both its fish and game, is one of the most prolific spots upon the Club's preserves. Its location between the mountains, and the excellent feeding grounds it affords for deer and moose, attract large numbers of these animals. The second-growth shrubbery (which deer are so fond of) upon each bank, and the tender plants floating in its waters, make it a favorite resort, while the adjacent thickly wooded mountains afford plenty of shelter. The writer has seen moose at two o'clock in the afternoon feeding in the open expanse at the head of the lake, and deer at any time from 4 P.M. to 8 A.M.; and many moose have been "laid low" in this particular spot. Next to the bogs in the Upper Spider River, Hathan Bog is the best place for moose in the region. The lower bog is also a favorite place for deer early in the season. Although a bog (so called), some of the finest trout ever tasted have been taken from its waters.

The trout in Hathan Bog are particularly fine flavored. always fat and plump ; and the fishing is good at any season or time of day. Although not large as a general rule, an occasional two-pounder is taken ; and sportsmen camping here can always be assured of plenty of trout to eat. The following places are the most prolific : at the narrows just at the foot of the open expanse in the upper bog, above and below each beaver dam, and for a distance of fifty rods along the lower end of the bog, from the boat landing up to where a small stream enters on the right ; in fact, almost anywhere where there is an opening in the lily-pads, sufficiently large to trail a fly, trout will be found. They have a decided preference for the "early worm," and immediately after daybreak is the best time to fish here. In the lower bog, although not so large a space, the fishing is even better than in the upper.

The favorite fishing hole here is from where the brook emptying Crosby Pond enters, up to the next curve in the bog, where a beautiful cold stream trickles in on the right hand side. This spot is about fifteen rods long, quite deep, and seems to have an inexhaustible supply of trout, running from one-half to three-quarters of a pound, upon the average. The pool is fringed on both sides with lily-pads, and must be approached very cautiously with the canoe, in order to produce no commotion in the water, and great sport may be expected. The best trout fishing ever experienced by the writer was in this pool, who was, presumably, the first to cast a fly on its waters. In writing a description of trout waters. one must be careful of the "shoals of understatement. and more particularly the quagmire of exaggeration"; but the trout in this pool, nevertheless, are a marvel. I am quite clear of the "quagmire" when I say, in making a cast with three flies, a dozen fine trout would rise from all quarters, and turn somersaults over

BREAKFAST IN THE LEAN-TO (between Hathan Bog and Crosby Pond).

the flies in their eagerness to bite, and, upon the first occasion of fishing in this pool, I accomplished the remarkable feat of bringing to net at one cast, with three flies, *four trout!* The guide assisted me in landing them; and the only way to explain the capture of the fourth trout was that it was scooped in by the net in landing the other three, although the smallest of the catch was over one-quarter of a pound. Only last season, some fine strings of trout were caught in this pool. Captain Hinman and myself caught in an evening's fishing one hundred and twelve trout, returning all to the water except twenty-two, which were over three-quarters of a pound each. Some of the catch can be seen in the illustration on the opposite page..

The record for trout fishing was broken in this pool last September, upon the occasion of the visit of a party from Boston, who camped in the vicinity for a couple of days. Among the party was the Club's attorney, Mr. Charles Hanks, and the writer. It was proposed that we take one of the guides, with a birch canoe, and visit this pool for an evening's fishing. The trail leading from our camp to the bog was a poor one, having become almost obliterated, on account of the high growth of the shrubbery, and the fallen, partially burnt logs also forming severe barriers to our progress with the canoe. The start was made at 3.30 P.M., and the bog reached at 4.45. The representative of the law, being pretty well disgusted with the tramp, declared that there was "not a trout in the entire mud hole." I offered a wager that we could easily catch one hundred trout before we returned, if they were in a biting humor, and the bet was eagerly taken by the barrister; but upon reflection, considering the lateness of the season, I made an amendment in this particular: that, if the trout would rise at all so as to take ten trout, I would catch seventy-five, and the amendment was accepted, but a "time limit" was placed upon me,— I was to land my trout before six o'clock; it was then 4.45.

I was conceded considerable "cheek" to make such a wager. "Seventy-five trout in an hour and a quarter!" But after arranging that the wager go to the guide, whichever side won, the "birch" was launched, and the guide directed to paddle quietly down to the pool. The first cast induced two or three trout to rise, and one was landed; the next cast seemed to set the waters boiling, and two trout were brought to net. Terror was plainly depicted upon the face of the legal man. At this time, I was casting just opposite where the cold stream flowed in, and having all the sport the most ardent angler could wish for; but the trout were running so large that considerable time was consumed in playing them, before they could be safely landed. Our attorney had conceded that I could land the seventy-five trout all right, but he was pretty sure he had me on the "time allowance." As there were no restrictions placed upon the size of the fish, I directed the guide to move a little lower down, away from the inlet, and gave the large trout a rest. Here they were smaller, and the numbers ran up rapidly, three at one cast being landed on two or three occasions. The guide was keeping tally, and held the watch. He called "time" at 5.54 (and six minutes to spare!), just as two half-pounders were landed. This made seventy-six trout caught, and in sixty-nine minutes! As all small trout had been carefully returned to the water, we paddled up stream again, and fished till time to return to camp and supper. The total number caught was one hundred and twenty-five. Besides returning all the small ones to the water, we carried a fifteen-pound creel, well filled, to the camp.

Besides this pool, there is good fishing all the way down to the dam; another very deep hole, where some large trout always lie, can be found about ten rods above the dam.

I might add that the favorite flies in both these waters are the Red Ibis, Queen of the Waters, and Brown Hackle (small hooks); but, if you want to allure larger trout, substitute Reuben Wood and

Lord Baltimore for the Queen of the Waters and Brown Hackle. I would be satisfied to go into the Upper Dead River region any time during July, August, and September, with only these six varieties, having a cast of each made up, and using them as above, according to the size the trout were running, although it is well to take along a few Professors, Blue Jays, and Grizzly Kings, and other varieties, to satisfy the more fastidious; but, keeping a record of the number of trout caught upon different varieties of flies, I must yield the palm to the Queen of the Waters for "pan fish" in this region, it standing at the head of the list by a large majority. Earlier in the season, during the month of June, the Parmachenee Belle is a very killing fly.

Hathan Bog is reached by a five-mile trail from White Birch Camp at Spider Lake. A good trail from the foot of the bog connects it with Crosby Pond less than half a mile distant. Another trail will be cut through, connecting the upper bog with the lower, a distance of three-quarters of a mile, and also from the bay in Crosby Pond, connecting with the lower bog less than a mile distant.

From the dam at the foot of the lower bog will be a trail a mile and a half in length, coming out at the forks of the Dead River.

There will be a small camp, a lean-to, at the head of the lower bog, for the convenience of members who go there for an evening and morning fishing. A large, commodious camp will be erected at Crosby Pond, to accommodate members while stopping at Hathan Bog, as there is no good site for a camp upon the bog, on account of the timber being burnt off and the land so marshy; while between the two waters nearest Crosby Pond is a fine knoll, offering every accommodation for a camp. Quite a show of wild ducks breed in both bogs, and there is good partridge shooting all along the different trails.

Hathan Bog, on account of its various attractions, must become a popular resort for members who wish to take a tramp back in the woods, rough it, and toast their toes in front of the log camp-fire, where

> Now there gleams
> The cheerful fire that lights the evening camp,
> Where weary sportsmen gather from their tramp
> To while away the hour, as one by one
> They tell adventures with the rod or gun.
> With mirth and song, with wit and humor bright,
> The time is passed, till all must say, "Good night,
> And pleasant dreams."

CROSBY POND,

So NAMED from a guide of that name in the Dead River region, is situated upon the Coburn Gore, between Hathan Bog and Arnold Pond, about a mile from the Canadian boundary. It is beautifully located, in a densely wooded region, the shores to the water's edge being fringed with heavy timber overhanging the water, with the exception of a few rods near the foot of the pond, opposite the Hathan Bog, which were included in the fire. It is the largest body of water up in the Gore, being over a mile long and half a mile wide. It is almost round in shape, containing a very pretty island in its center. The illustration on page 69 is from a photograph taken from the head of the pond, near the inlet, and shows the island and the mountains in the distance (south) forming the valley in which lies the Chain of Ponds proper. A more secluded romantic spot to camp in cannot be found anywhere in the territory. The water is clear and cold, and contains both speckled and lake trout. The largest speckled trout in the region are to be found in Crosby Pond, but like all large trout they only rise to the fly at certain times. During these times, the trout will average four to five pounds. Small trout, from one-quarter of a pound to a pound in weight, will rise to the fly almost any time at the head of the lake. Crosby Pond is full of minnows, which probably accounts for the trout not rising to a fly, which may possibly be remedied by restocking with small fry, without putting in the usual quota of "bait fish," and thus giving the trout predominance. The lake undoubtedly contains fine trout, and is well worthy of a trial; and on account of its proximity to Hathan Bog, and the excellent facilities afforded for camping, it is sure to become a favorite resort. Deer come down to its shores to drink and escape from the flies, and in the summer season can be seen almost any morning or evening; but, as the law is not off in Maine till October, not many can be shot, as by that time there is plenty of water for them in the forests. A camp owned by Mr. Wells, of New York, is built on the west shore, just opposite where the Club camp will be located. Trails connect this pond with Hathan Bog (one-half mile), Rush Lake (six miles), Arnold Pond (one and one-quarter mile), and Horseshoe Pond (one mile); and it is quite possible a direct trail will be cut through from Spider Lake, passing along the west side of Louise Mountain, the trail from Spider Lake to Hathan Bog passing along the east base of the mountain, as shown upon the map. I might add that, in fishing for the large speckled trout in this pond, I have found the Polka, Blue Jay, Full-winged Ibis, Lord Baltimore, and Reuben Wood very killing flies. Such as are fond of angling with worms and a long line and sinker can catch trout, that will run from half a pound to one pound in weight, just off the rocky ledge point near the camp; and no one who chooses to adopt this method of fishing need go hungry while camping there. This and Arnold Pond are favorite waters for loons; and as they destroy a lot of fish, and there is no law against shooting them, they make good targets, and afford considerable amusement for all who have plenty of ammunition to waste upon them.

Between Crosby Pond and the Lower Hathan Bog, and covering about ten acres of land, lies a small marshy mud hole, rejoicing in the euphonious name of

CROSBY POND (looking south).

CRANBERRY BOG.

It does not contain any fish, to the knowledge of the writer, but is quite a resort for game, on account of the good feeding grounds along its banks. Should the month of September become an open month for shooting deer in Maine, no better place than this could be found to lie concealed and watch for deer to come out and feed, as a rifle at any point along the bog would command the entire feeding grounds.

As deer do not come into the water to feed very much after October 1, this bog is of very little importance.

ARNOLD POND AND THE CHAIN OF PONDS.

HIS beautiful sheet of water takes its name from General Benedict Arnold, who crossed the pond (which is about one and one-quarter miles long) in bateaux, with his troops and "implements of war," upon the occasion of his memorable expedition against Quebec. The water lies two miles north of Massachusetts Bog, and between it and Mud Pond, and is the largest body of water in the upper chain, with the exception of Crosby Pond. It is by far the prettiest sheet of water upon the Coburn Gore, is about half a mile from the boundary, and lies at the base of Black Mountain, upon its northern shore. The pond, on account of its resemblance to a moose horn in shape, has been put down on maps as Moose Horn Pond.

In the northwestern corner of the pond is a fine point projecting out, covered with pine trees.—Point of Pines,—upon which there is a beautiful site for camping. A camp has been built near by, and put in order and furnished by the Club, for the accommodation of its members. Fishing in the pond has not been particularly good the last few years, on account of its proximity to the settlement of Wooburn; and it has been suspected that nets have been freely used in its waters. Formerly, both speckled and lake trout were very abundant, and late reports say the trout are upon the increase again.

It is a most delightful place to camp, and with a little restocking will become a popular place for sportsmen, as game of all kind is plentiful in the vicinity. It was here that the headquarters of the

ARNOLD POND.

party who slaughtered so many deer in the winter of 1884–85 were made. Two thousand eight hundred pounds of venison — hind-quarters only — were shipped out to the Boston market. The deer were all killed in the vicinity of Arnold Pond, extending southward to Massachusetts Bog, and northward along the boundary line.

In spite of this tremendous drain, deer are increasing rapidly about here. The writer camped at Arnold Pond the week between Christmas and New Year's last, in company with Colonel Harrington, of Boston, and, in tramping across from the pond to Crosby (a little over a mile distant), came upon over seventy places where deer had lain overnight since the last fall of snow, some three or four days previous.

Trails connect this pond with Massachusetts Bog (south), the boundary line (west), Mud Pond (fifty rods to eastward), and with Crosby Pond, the latter trail going in at the head of the bay in the northeast corner, and coming out near the outlet of Crosby Pond (less than one and a half miles).

Next to Arnold Pond, in an easterly direction, lies

Mud Pond,

a small rocky pond, sometimes called Rock or Round Pond. It is round in shape, covered with lily-pads, which greatly interfere with the fishing. The pond contains speckled trout, but is not much fished, on account of the abundant growth of lily-pads. It is a favorite feeding ground for deer, and is a fine pond for jacking or still-hunting. The brook between it and Arnold contains large numbers of small trout. Less than a quarter of a mile to the east, upon the same stream, is

A DOMESTICATED DEER (Arnold Pond Camp).

HORSESHOE POND,

much larger than Mud Pond, and well stocked with trout,— it is in shape somewhat like a horseshoe,— and at the foot of the pond is a dam for driving logs, constructed by Messrs. M. G. Shaw & Sons, who own the adjacent township. Very good fishing at times can be had in this pond, and below the dam, the fish resembling very much those in Big Northwest Pond, while deer frequent the place all through the summer. A trail continues past this pond from Arnold, extending southeasterly to the Chain of Ponds proper and Eustis, following the Old Tote Road. There is no camp located here, as the pond can be reached in less than a quarter of an hour's tramp from Arnold. A trail leads from Horseshoe, the northern shore, to the outlet of Crosby Pond, about a mile distant.

From here the Dead River takes a southeasterly course across the Chain of Ponds township, the Gore Stream branch being joined by the stream emptying Crosby Pond and the Hathan Bog at a point about two miles above Round Pond (the first of the Chain of Ponds proper). There is good fishing in this stream, particularly between Hathan Bog and the forks, as in places are to be found deep holes and flumes in the rocks well stocked with large trout, and few parties ever fish in them, as they are out of the general route in this region.

A short distance below the forks is a small stream coming in from

OTTER POND,

a very pretty little pond with high rocky shores. It is reached the easiest from Horseshoe Pond, but up to the present time no trail has been cut through to it. It is said to contain a goodly supply of speckled

WINTER SCENE ON ARNOLD POND. (From a Photograph.)

trout; but, as the writer has never cast a fly upon its waters, he is unable to give a practical account of its qualities as a fish pond. The

CHAIN OF PONDS PROPER

comprises, in order: Round, Long, Beaver, Bag, and Lower Ponds. Round Pond covers about fifty acres of land, and affords good fishing. A boat can be run into Long Pond through the narrows, which are only a few rods long. Long Pond is the largest and prettiest of the chain, is about three miles long and of varying width. It contains both speckled and lake trout; and the fishing is very good, particularly near the foot of the pond, where the Indian Stream empties in. Large numbers of fish are caught through the ice in the winter season, in this pond.

The scenery about the pond is very fine. Upon the east shore is a high rocky ledge on the side of the mountain, nearly overhanging the lake, while upon all sides are ranges of mountains.

This place is of interest, not only on account of Arnold's trip through here, but also on account of a foul murder perpetrated,

Long Pond, "Chain of Ponds."

some twenty years ago, upon the shore of Long Pond. The victim was an Indian girl, a sister of Joe Marie, the celebrated Indian guide at Megantic. The murderer, a white man, after committing the crime, threw the body into the lake, where it was found floating upon the water by some lumbermen, and buried a few days after by a couple of Maine guides. A rude cedar-post marks the resting-place of the unfortunate victim, whose murder has never been avenged, the grave lying upon the small neck of land intervening between Round and Long Ponds. Next below Long Pond, and lying to the eastward, is Beaver Pond, and next in order comes Bag, then Lower Pond, all containing more or less trout, and connected by short streams, navigable with small boats. These ponds are connected by a trail (Shaw's Tote Road), which runs upon the west shore, with Arnold Pond (northward) and Eustis, and a number of lumber camps are to be found at different points along the trail. Messrs. Shaw have a nice camp upon the Indian Stream, and Peter LeRoyer has a good camp at the head of Long Pond. Game is very plentiful all along the valley of this Chain of Ponds, and no better ground can be found for still-hunting. The trip in a canoe down this pond to Eustis is a most enjoyable one. It was in this vicinity that Peter LeRoyer, the well-known Indian guide, caught and domesticated a young moose, which he drives about and works like a horse. The animal is now four years old, and as tame and quiet as any ox, occasionally straying into the woods, but always returning again.

"Tommy," the tame Moose.

MASSACHUSETTS BOG.

ETWEEN three and four miles north of Big Northwest Pond, the most remote of the Seven Ponds group, and between it and Arnold Pond, lies a dilatation of the Gore Stream (a branch of the Dead River), named Massachusetts Bog. Its original name — Caribou Bog — was given it by Mr. Kennedy Smith; but it was changed to its present name by a party of sportsmen from Boston, who, on account of its wonderful and almost inexhaustible supply of speckled trout, honored it with the name of their native State. It is a question whether the palm belongs to this bog or Northwest Pond for the best fishing in the region. Presumably, Massachusetts Bog contains a larger number, but the fish will average larger in Northwest Pond. Both waters are upon the township leased by the Club from Messrs. Hazeltine, Knowlton, and Hall, of Belfast, Me., the same lease also comprising Grant, Little Northwest, and the South Boundary Ponds.

The bog lies at the base of the Boundary Mountains upon the Maine side, and, running in a winding course parallel to them, is over a mile and a half long, but at no place over three hundred feet wide. The illustration is from a view taken about midway the bog. During the summer months there is only a narrow channel in places not covered with lily-pads, and it is in these clear places, where there is an opportunity to cast a fly, that the trout rise so well. This bog is widely known for its excellent fishing, the trout rising all through the season and at any time of the day. One is always assured of good sport at Massachusetts Bog. The trout are not large, but will average in the best season of the year half a pound, while an occasional trout weighing as high as a pound and a half or two pounds is taken. Four pound trout have been caught here.

There is little doubt that the bog still contains large trout, although it has been the writer's misfortune to find them average smaller than others report. The following very interesting letter from our Vice-President, Mr. Woodruff, of New York, anent this subject, shows what fish have been taken out, and within the last three years. The story of his success has often been told in the region as a "fish story"; but, being a little incredulous, the writer asked Mr. Woodruff for the facts of the case, and lately received the following letter, dated New York, July 16, 1887 : —

> *My dear Doctor,*— Absence from the city for a few days has prevented an earlier reply to your last. You say that you have heard some tall stories from Mose and Joe Noel about a certain day's fishing I had at Massachusetts Bog, and ask me to give you *my* account of it. You are very careful, however, I notice, not to say what the tenor and "size" of these stories are; hence, as guides are proverbial at drawing the long bow or — should I say in this case? — making a long cast. I will simply give you a plain, unvarnished tale.
>
> We had our camp that season, you will remember, at Point of Pines, on Arnold Pond. For three weeks we had whipped Beaver Brook, Arnold, Horseshoe, Rock, Upper and Lower Hathan, Cranberry, and had even tried Mud Pond, with but fair success, while our ears were constantly being filled with tales of the big trout in Massachusetts Bog, and the monsters taken out of there through the ice the previous winter. But, whenever we spoke of going there, we were told of the white cedar swamps, three hours to get there, too far to go and return the same day, no camp there, and so on, until every tale was taken *cum grano salis*; and most of our party left on the first of September without having essayed the bog, leaving only my brother, nephew, and myself in camp. The next day, happening to be on the top of Black Mountain with Mose, he called my attention to a little patch of water, about as large as your two palms, two miles off, as the crow flies, which he said was Massachusetts Bog. One glance at the lay

of the land, and all fear of white cedar swamps vanished from my mind; and the next morning I started with him for the much-talked-of spot. Going directly across from Point of Pines, I took the ridge on the left of the brook until it ran into the swamp, which we crossed at a spot only a few hundred feet wide, and then took the hard wood ridge again on the right, much to the disgust of Mose, who wanted to follow the "blaze" made in winter, on snow-shoes, through the swamp the whole way. I think he predicted that, if I kept on in my course, I would come out at Northwest Pond. However, when I left the ridge at right angles and, turning to the left, plunged down into the valley, my good luck was again with me, and we struck the bog just where the brook enters it, thus placing myself as high in the estimation of Mose for my knowledge of woodcraft as my lucky long shot that first season at a buck forever perched me on the highest pinnacle in Joe's estimation as a crack rifle shot.

I had my rod and little Stevens rifle, while Mose had only his inseparable axe and a small parcel of grub. It was now about three in the afternoon, and our first thought was to find the boat, which Mose had cached that spring, and which he said was essential in order to get any trout. After an hour's fruitless search, Mose "remembered" that the Indian — What was his name,— the one who had the cow moose? — had been told where the boat was; and, as he had been there a few weeks before, *ergo* the boat must be at the "other end." The quickest way to get to the "other end" was to make a bee line through the white cedar swamp, Mose said. Leaving coats and rod where we *intended* to spend the night, taking only the little rifle and axe, Mose took the lead through the swamp. If you have never been through that bit of white cedar in a wet season, then I can only give you *Punch's* famous advice, "Don't," — words fail me even at this length of time to do justice to it. It was after six when we got to that "other end," wet through to the skin, half fresh and half salt water. By seven o'clock we had decided that the boat was not at the "other end." It was too late to get back to camp, it was rapidly growing cold, for you know how cold the nights often are up there early in September, and there was nothing for us to do but make a fire, dry our garments, and lie down on the bare ground, with the leaves for our bedspread, the stars for our canopy, and empty stomachs for an early rising alarm clock. We had even left three partridges at the camp, which I had shot on the way over. I recall how Mose complained only at his not having put a handful of tea in his pocket. Between the water from below and the perspiration from above, it would have been in a fine condition, though, doubtless, he would have found no fault with it, and I question if I should have "made a fuss over such a trifle." But the fun began after dark. Mose made a roaring fire on the edge of the bluff, and we steamed and scorched one side while we slapped the other to keep it from congealing, until we were partially dry. Then lying down on our arms we waited for the stars to roll around. About midnight all the bears in the State of Maine seemed to have congregated on the mountain back of us, and the roaring, grunting, and squealing I never heard equaled in any menagerie. Sleep under any circumstances would have been difficult in our case, with that infernal racket it was impossible. With every fresh outburst, Mose would jump to his feet, mutter something about "dam bear," throw more wood on the fire, until the flames leaped twenty feet in the air, and then chop away until he had replenished his pile for the next stoking, keeping it up until the whole thing became ludicrous to me. Every little while there would be the stamp, snort, and indignant whistle, on the opposite shore, of some deer kept from wetting the aforesaid whistle by the bright light of our protective fire. But all disagreeable as well as good things finally come to an end; and the first clear gleam of daylight saw us wending our way back, this time on the ridge, even Mose having had enough of the swamp. After demolishing all the grub we had brought with us, and soothing our injured feelings with several pipes, I took a nap while Mose hunted up the boat. About ten o'clock he woke me by saying he saw the boat adrift on the tamarack swamp side of the bog. Taking my rod, I went about one hundred yards down the bog, where there was a grassy bank, and proceeded to "limber up," to be in readiness when Mose came with the boat. But Mose, who could never get over the mystery of putting a rod together, stayed to see the operation. I had that heavy English rod—pole, it should almost be called—and the famous blue silk line, both of which you probably remember. Having adjusted my leader, I let the flies fall in the water at my feet, where it was not more than a foot deep. As I stepped back to take hold of the butt of my rod, z-z-z-z-i-p-p-p went the reel, and a few moments later Mose was taking off a fourteen-inch trout, which had had the impudence to take a fly within a foot of the bank. With three flies on, the first cast hooked two beauties, and the next cast gave me one on each fly. Nothing but the toughness of that heavy old rod and the strength of the silk line enabled me to land the whole party. I then took off two of the flies, and at every cast, standing in full sight on the bank, five to ten trout would throw themselves completely out of the water, and I had such trout fishing as I never even dreamed of. Mose, standing in the water up to his knees, would land them, and take them off the hook, and toss them into a little pool back of him. I had no idea of the time, never having to make a second cast for a fish. but striking a big fellow every time, until Mose said, "How much feesh you want, Monsieur Vood?" As I looked around, the pool was filled to overflowing with such a pile of golden beauties as Fulton Market never knew. There was not a fish under fourteen inches in length, and from that up to twenty-two inches for the longest. But such misshapen fellows as some of them were, the under jaw projecting far over the upper,— regular beaks; others with a corporation on them which would have done honor to a member of the Fat Men's Club. Upon looking at my watch, it was a quarter past twelve. I had been fishing about two hours. On counting the catch, we had one hundred and thirty-seven trout. My heart smote me for taking so many, but we had carried them up to camp before counting them, and it was too late to put any of them back then. So we did the best we could to prevent willful waste, by gutting them. building a smoke house, and giving what we could not eat that day a smoking all that afternoon, night, and until noon the next day, when we started back for Arnold. Mose had all the "pack" he wanted, and said he had fully seventy-five pounds in weight. On showing them to my brother, I was pleasantly greeted with the announcement that one rod could not have caught all that quantity in the short time stated, and asked how large a *net* Mose had. Two days later, my brother and nephew went over to Massachusetts with me, reaching there about noon. All that afternoon the three rods were whipping the bog from one end to the other, from the shore and from the boat, and not a single fish could any of us obtain. *Nets* of all kinds were the staple of conversation around the camp fire that night. Needless to say that Mose and I took no interest or part in the conversation. But the next morning. before the others were up. I slipped down to the spot where I had caught all the first lot, and the first cast gave me a stunner, tipping the scales at four and one-quarter pounds. I woke the others up by flapping the cold tail in their faces. Inside of half an hour they took back all they had said about *nets*, and they only ceased catching the big fellows, which seem to be the only kind in that bog, because we did not know what we should do with them. As it was, we sent in, or rather took in with us to Montreal, as we broke up camp the next day, close on to one hundred pounds of half-smoked trout, which were a great treat to our friends there, but who wondered why we did not seem to care much for them.

Such is my experience at Massachusetts Bog. If you want to know why, the afternoon of the first day my brother was there, we could not get a single rise. I can only say that trout, like some women, are "queer critters." I have heard since the most contradictory stories about this spot, some parties praising it in the most extravagant manner, while others will declare that there is not a single trout in the bog. Of one thing I am certain, there are no small trout there, and the question is, What will we do when all these big ones are yanked out? Another thing, I did not see a single dark colored trout taken from the bog, all of them being the handsome golden striped trout, with flesh of an unusually dark pink tint.

Now let me know how my plain, ungarnished tale compares with what you heard from Mose and Joe Noel. I expect to see the boys next month, when I shake off the dust of the city for a month in the greenwood, and, if they have said anything to stagger my reputation, I want to know it in time to get even with them.

Trusting to meet you at White Birch Camp some time next month, and . . . I am

Very truly yours,

I. O. WOODRUFF.

In fishing in this pond, sportsmen should be careful to return to the water all trout under eight inches in length, as plenty of half and three-quarter pound trout can be taken to supply the camp for a large party in an evening or morning's fishing; and with proper care the fishing in the bog can be made even better, and the trout average larger. The writer has seen at one time the sickening sight of nearly a bushel of trout of all sizes piled upon the shore at the landing, in a state of decay, that had been caught by vandals who did not know enough to return to the water all except those needed for the fry-pan. Such wanton destruction of fish is most unwarrantable, and no gentlemen worthy the name of sportsmen would ever allow it, but would check the enthusiasm of any member in their party who could not stop after catching enough for present wants, or, if the sport were persisted in, would compel him to return carefully to the water all the trout he might land; for, by so doing, the same trout, in a more

MASSACHUSETTS BOG (central portion).

developed state, would furnish sport for others. And, in a place where fish are so plentiful, there is no excuse for the killing of trout under one-half pound in weight, unless the party is large, and the trout happen to be running small.

One can have excellent sport, and secure all the trout needed for food, by taking in a small pair of spring balances, and not killing a single trout unless he brings the springs down to one-half, three-quarters, or even a pound, according to the location when fishing; and, if members of the Club would adopt this plan, we could always be sure of good fishing. The taking of a few of the largest trout, needed for the immediate wants of camping parties, will not have a perceptible effect upon the fishing; but it is the killing of so many small trout that depletes the ponds.

Apart from its excellent fishing record, Massachusetts Bog enjoys the reputation of being the best resort for deer of any of the ponds or bogs in the Upper Dead River or Seven Ponds regions, during the summer months; but the law makes it expensive to kill a deer before the first of October. It is very pleasant to watch them come out upon the edges of the bog during the day; and, if all firearms are left in the camp, one can go out in the evening with a jack-light, and watch their movements. Often while fishing in the early morning or after sunset, the click of the reel will startle a deer which has been quietly feeding near by, and a whistle will be the first indication that game is at hand.

One of the finest camps in the territory has lately been built at this place by the Club, and named "Camp Massachusetts." It is twenty feet wide and thirty feet long, made of spruce logs peeled. The camp is furnished with a range and complete cooking utensils and camp furniture. It is located upon the stream emptying the bog and flowing into Arnold Pond, about fifty rods from the foot of the bog, the location being made here on account of a beautiful never-failing spring of clear cold water, and also on account of using the camp for still-hunting in the fall, as in that case it is not desirable to be located immediately upon the bog. A good trail connects the camp with the bog, and a trail has been cut from Gagné's (at the end of the buckboard road), where the Old Tote Road crosses from Canada into Maine, through to the camp, about two miles distant, so that a horse can be taken in with supplies, etc., or take the "tenderfoot" from the buckboard to the camp.

There are also two small lean-to's upon the hill, to the right of the trail, that will accommodate half a dozen or more, also another lean-to at the head of the bog, at the commencement of the trail leading to Big Northwest Pond.

On account of the excellent locality thereabouts for deer, Camp Massachusetts will be a general rendezvous for still-hunting parties in the fall of the year. The Club has already got a fine clinker-built boat in this bog, and a canoe, and more boats will be added during the present season.

The months of August and early September are probably the best time for fishing in this place, but one can be assured of good fishing here all through the season.

THE SEVEN PONDS.

 T is hard to find a locality more beautifully situated in such a wild picturesque region, and with such a wealth of fish and game as is offered by the Seven Ponds. Although called the Seven Ponds, this group consists of not less than ten ponds; namely, Big Island, Little Island, Rock, L. Grant, Big Northwest, Little Northwest, South Boundary, Beaver, and Long Pond. A radius of less than two miles from Grant Pond will take in the entire group. They form the headwaters of two different rivers, the Northwests and Boundary Ponds flowing north into the Gore Stream (Dead River), while the remainder flow in a southerly direction into the Kennebago Stream (Androscoggin River). All of the ponds are connected with good trails, and most of them have boats and camps, built by guides in that region, and more particularly by Mr. Kennedy Smith, of Eustis, Me., who has besides gone to a great expense in laying out a road into the ponds. These ponds are all noted for their sure fishing during the entire season, and disappointment in the number and size of the trout has never been experienced here. Approaching the ponds from the Canadian boundary along the Club preserves, the first one along the route is

BIG NORTHWEST POND,

situated about three and a half miles south from Massachusetts Bog. In size it is about the third largest in the group, and nearly round in shape. It is fed by a couple of small brooks, and receives the waters from Little Northwest and South Boundary Ponds. The trail from Massachusetts Bog comes out near the outlet in the north end of the pond. A trail also connects it at the opposite end with Grant Pond, one-quarter of a mile distant. Upon the west side is the Boundary range of mountains, the highest being Mount Gosford, which is quite close to the pond. Two very comfortable camps, with open fireplaces, are situated on the southwestern shore, built three or four years ago by some Rangeley guides.— Messrs. Snowman, Haines, Crosby, and Twombly,— who also put in four or five good boats, and went to considerable expense and trouble in opening up the place for the accommodation of sport-men, before the territory was leased to the Club. The camps are delightfully situated, giving a view of Snow Mountain and Boil to the eastward. The fishing in this pond is considered the best of all the ponds in the group, although the trout do not average as large as in Big Island and L.; but, for numbers and positive results, Big Northwest Pond must be yielded the palm. The trout do not rise more readily here than in Massachusetts Bog, but it excels the latter in producing a larger average in size. The following score, made by the writer and Mr. Fred. A. Foster, of Boston, during a few days' fishing in these ponds in the month of June last, will give an idea of the sport experienced here : —

						CAUGHT.	KILLED.
Monday,	June	6 (evening),	Massachusetts Bog			60	14
Tuesday,	"	7 (morning),	"	"		30	10
"	"	7 (evening),	"	"		75	15
Wednesday,	"	8 "	Big Northwest Pond			90	10
Thursday,	"	9 (morning),	"	"		50	8
"	"	9 (evening),	Big Island Pond			15	2

			CAUGHT.	KILLED.
Friday,	June 10 (morning), Big Island Pond		14	4
"	" 10 (evening), L Pond		68	2
Saturday,	" 11 (morning), Rock and Grant Ponds		17	0
"	" 11 (evening), Big Northwest Pond		49	15
Monday,	" 13 (morning), Little Island Pond		38	3
"	" 13 (evening), Big Northwest Pond		75	15
			381	98

There is a peculiarity about the trout in Big Northwest Pond worth mentioning. Nearly all the trout will be found to contain small pigmentary spots mingled with the colored spots. Many sportsmen look upon them with suspicion, and think the trout unclean on this account; but it does not make the slightest difference in the flavor of the trout, the spots are simply skin deep. The cause is unknown; the peculiarity is confined to this pond, although an occasional one is taken out of Massachusetts Bog, and quite often out of Horseshoe Pond.

Although the trout did not run large,— one pound nine ounces being the largest one taken,— they made up in numbers; very few trout were hooked under half a pound. Only enough were saved to supply the camp, all the rest being carefully returned to the water as soon as caught. Many of the trout thrown back were pounders, and over, especially of those caught in Big Island Pond. An estimate of the size of those killed can be made by considering that the ninety-eight supplied the camp with fish for eight days (two of these days the party numbered six, the remainder of the time three, with appetites at no time very delicate). A good deal of our success was due to the excellent judgment of our guide, Mr.

Martin Fuller, of Eustis, Me., who is probably the oldest guide in this region, having guided about these ponds continuously for fourteen years, knowing exactly all the favorite haunts of the trout, their habits, and the most taking flies for that time of year, and locality. Big Northwest Pond is also a great place for deer. Upon the trip in question, in two days, we saw three deer come out, and were paddled up by our skillful guide within thirty feet of one of them in broad daylight. From the camps two trails lead out, one to the right, connecting with LITTLE NORTHWEST POND, and the other, at the left, with SOUTH BOUNDARY POND, neither of them over a quarter of a mile from the camps. They are sometimes called the Boundary Ponds; they are quite small, but important, on account of their being frequented so much by deer, the shore being dotted all the season by their tracks. They both contain trout. Less than a quarter of a mile to the southeast lies

GRANT POND,

a small round body of water, almost completely covered with lily-pads, but containing the fattest and finest flavored trout in the Seven Ponds. The fishing is a little uncertain in this pond; at times, the trout rise readily, then, again, one can whip the whole pond without a rise. Many sportsmen report "the best fishing they ever had" in Grant Pond, and it is well worthy of trials when camping at Big Northwest, which is the center and headquarters for the four ponds described. A trail connects this pond with Big Island (one and one-quarter miles) and Little Island (one and one-quarter miles), the one leading to Little Island being the general route to Kennebago Lake, and starts in a short distance down the right hand shore from the end of the Northwest trail. Big Island trail is upon the opposite shore. A good boat will be found upon the pond. Going south, the next sheet of water reached is

Grant Pond.

LITTLE ISLAND,

so named from the small island in it, which in the summer time is almost an isthmus, connected with the shore by long reeds and rushes. It is a very pretty pond, within sight of Boil and one of the Five Round Mountains to the east, with White Cap and the Boundary Mountains to the west. The fishing is very fine, as it is out of the way of the general route of sportsmen, and few trout are ever taken out of it. There are two boats upon the pond, but the camps are located nearly half a mile to the south, upon the shores of

BEAVER POND,

a small T shaped pond, but filled with trout, as all these ponds are. Upon the southern shore, opposite the camps, is a trail leading to

LONG POND,

the most southerly of the group, a long narrow creek; and from here the trail descends the Kennebago Stream to the lake, some twenty miles distant. The camps at Beaver Pond are the property of Messrs. Grant & Richardson, the proprietors of the Kennebago House, who have fitted them up with stoves, cooking utensils, dishes, blankets, and boats. The guides in this territory are privileged to use them,—a small rental, which is very reasonable, being expected when occupied by a party. From the head of Long Pond is a trail a little over a mile long, leading in an easterly direction to

L POND,

which is only a few rods from Big Island. This is one of the favorite ponds of the group, and the second largest in size,—it is in shape like the letter L,—lying at the base of Boil Mountain, and in close proximity to the Five Round Mountains and Snow Mountain. The trout in this pond are very fine and gamy, and will average about three-quarters of a pound, and run from that up to two pounds. It is a rare occurrence to hook a trout less than one-half pound in this pond. The bottom is very rocky, covered with ledges, and the water cold and clear. The best fishing ground is at the elbow and opposite the boat landing. Mr. Kennedy Smith has a number of boats upon the pond; and an old camp, built by

Mr. Douglas, of Eustis, used to stand near the landing, but a large tree in falling completely destroyed it, so that it is now unused. About as far north of Big Island as L Pond is south of it, lies

Rock Pond,

a small triangular body of water, connected by a trail with Big Island. It affords pretty good fishing. Boats belonging to the camps at Big Island are to be found on the pond. A trail also connects this pond with Massachusetts Bog, joining the Northwest trail about midway between the two ponds.

By far the largest and most beautiful of all the Seven Ponds group is

Big Island Pond.

No better description of this charming place can be given than that written in the excellent little "Guide Book to the Dead River Region," published by Mr. A. W. Robinson, of Boston, which is given *verbatim*: —

"On entering the clearing from the wood road, over which the trip from Tim Pond has been made, seven log-cabins are discovered scattered around beneath the overhanging trees. These cabins are even better than those at Tim Pond, and are furnished the same, while the large dining-cabin, which is located near the center of the clearing, is very tastily decorated, and the table all that could be desired.

"A cold spring supplies the camp with water, and a short distance from it a small brook has been dammed, and conveniences for keeping live trout arranged.

"The clearing, the work of Mr. Smith, is situated at the southeastern end of the pond, on a slight elevation, from which one of the finest views of this sheet of water and its surroundings is obtained.

"Stretching out before you a distance of three miles are its blue ruffled waters, broken here and there by some huge ledge which rises above the surface, while the surrounding forests closely line the rough and rocky shores.

"Towering above the camp on the east is Snow Mountain, one of the highest peaks in Maine. It can be ascended from the camp; but as its sides are covered to the summit with a thick growth of spruce, hemlock, and pine trees, the trip is very arduous, and it is hardly safe to attempt it without a guide, as there are no paths to aid a stranger. The view from the summit is grand, as the surrounding country can be seen for miles, and on a fair day the steamer on Lake Megantic can be discerned with the naked eye.

"Looking down the pond from the camp, the Boundary Mountains stretch along the horizon, and the rounded slopes of Boil Mountain are visible at the south.

"One is enthused with new life as he breathes the pure air and feasts his eyes on the beauties of nature, spread like a panorama everywhere around.

"The trout in these waters are larger than in the rest of the ponds, and are very plenty, it not being an uncommon thing for an expert angler to land twenty-five or thirty pounds in a short time.

"The best fishing grounds are near the island and in the numerous coves around the shore, where mountain streams pour their cold waters into the pond.

"For fly-fishing, the months of June and July are the best; but the trout rise through the entire season, the most taking fly being the Red Ibis. For deep fishing, the angler will find an excellent bait in the shape of a small fish which the guides call a chub, and with which the pond is stocked; this bait is also used for trolling, and, as the law forbids the use of a 'spoon,' it will be found a very good substitute."

Partridge Nest.

The writer can heartily indorse what Mr. Robinson has said of Big Island Pond, and a more comfortable place to stop, and enjoy fishing and hunting, than Kennedy Smith's camps is hard to find. There are now eleven camps, nicely fitted up with substantial camp furniture, including stoves, which are always comfortable during the evenings all through the season, and fragrant bough beds, while the dining camp is run equal to any of the first-class hotels in this region. Members of the Club, and sportsmen in general, will always find these camps a pleasant adjunct to their trip while in the Dead River region. Mr. Edgar Smith, who has charge of the camps for Mr. Viles, the present proprietor, will be found very obliging and painstaking with all his guests. The cost of living here is $2.00 per day.

Partridge photographed on its Nest.

including a private cabin and boats, the price for guide's board being $1.00 per day. The buckboard road from Tim Pond comes out here, notice of which will be taken in the chapter upon routes, etc.

At the head of Big Island Pond, and between it and Rock Pond, are situated the camps of Mr. John W. Mason, of New York, one of the Club's directors. They are the most elaborate camps in the region. Mr. Jean Soule, the well-known guide, is in charge of them.

From the Seven Ponds, a very pleasant trip can be taken down the Kennebago Stream to the lakes lying south of the Club preserves, and sportsmen contemplating this trip should provide themselves with Robinson's "Guide to the Dead River," which gives an excellent map and description of the region, including the Rangeley, Kennebago, Parmachenee, and

Bigelow Lakes. In fishing in the Seven Ponds, the following varieties of flies will be found the best to take in: During the month of June, Parmachenee Belle, Red Ibis, Queen of the Waters, Coachman, and Montreal; in July, Silver Doctor, Gold Doctor, the different Hackles (Brown, Ibis, Grizzly, etc.), Yellow May. Blue Jay, Jennie Lind, Professor, and Green Drake; in August, the Grizzly King, Yellow May, Silver Doctor, Reuben Wood, and Lord Baltimore; in September, the June flies take well, including Red Ibis, Cowdung, Parmachenee Belle. and Montreal.

The Queen of the Waters will be found a standard fly all through the season. At some of the fishing tackle stores, the Queen of the Waters will not be found. If sportsmen cannot get it tied for them, the Abbey will be found an excellent substitute, the resemblance between the two being very close.

MOOSE RIVER REGION.

 HIS tract of territory lies to the east of the international boundary, the headwaters of the Moose River arising just across the Canadian line. It comprises some ten or fifteen townships in Franklin County, extending from the boundary to Moosehead Lake, and embracing the different tributaries of the Moose River, and a dozen or fifteen lakes. The Canadian Pacific Railway runs through the entire region, the road being already graded half-way to Moosehead Lake, and by the ensuing fall will be completed, and the rails laid to the lake.

It is a most prolific region for large game and trout, but, on account of its being so easy of access, the sport must soon deteriorate, although there are still a number of small lakes almost unknown; and, if the country could only be judiciously protected, a most valuable preserve could be assured for years to come.

All the streams and ponds teem with speckled beauties; and no better region could be found for the canoeist and sportsman tourist, as the region for over fifty miles can be run through with a canoe, with very few portages. Small ponds completely dot the territory, commencing at the Canadian boundary and extending to Lake Brassua, the last in the chain before reaching Moosehead. Among the ponds now mostly frequented are Boundary Pond, Holeb and Attean Ponds, quite near the rails, and the main stream of the Moose River, which are all quite easy of access. The number of sportsmen going into this region is increasing daily; and, although the "iron horse", penetrates the region, an occasional moose is seen on the track even, and a case is reported, the present season, of one measuring its speed with the engine.

A construction train leaves the village of Megantic every morning at six o'clock, going to the end of the rails; and, although the contractors do not care particularly to "bother" with passengers, all sportsmen going into the region are courteously treated and given what accommodations there are. The train returns to the lake every evening, getting in between six and seven o'clock.

A most delightful trip, and one now quite often indulged in, is to take along a birch canoe and launch it in the river, and proceed down stream, camping at various stages, and fishing at the inlets of the numerous tributaries,— very few portages are necessary; and the trip can be extended to Moosehead Lake and down the Penobscot River to Bangor. A trip of this sort would use up about a fortnight, and would afford great sport in the way of fishing.

ROUTES, FARES, GUIDES, ETC.

 WE have our choice of two main thoroughfares in going to Megantic and the Dead River; namely, by the Boston & Lowell System and International Railway, or by the Maine Central and Franklin & Megantic Railways.

Each route has its various attractions. From New York, the Shore Line is a very comfortable route, and enables members to be joined by other parties at Boston, while the trip over the Connecticut River Road is very charming, and by going this way one can take the Pullman at Springfield, and not change till Sherbrooke is reached in the morning.

New York members can take the route as follows: —

Leave New York (N.Y., N.H. & H. R.R.)	4.30 P.M.
Arrive Springfield " " "	7.57 "
Leave Springfield (Connecticut River R.R.)	8.15 "
" Wells River Junction (Passumpsic R.R.)	2.00 A.M.
Arrive Newport, Vt. " "	4.15 "
Leave Newport " "	6.00 "
Arrive Sherbrooke, P.Q. " "	7.45 "
Leave Sherbrooke (International R'y) (Saturdays, 3.30 P.M.)	3.00 P.M.
Arrive Lake Megantic " " " 6.30 "	8.00 "

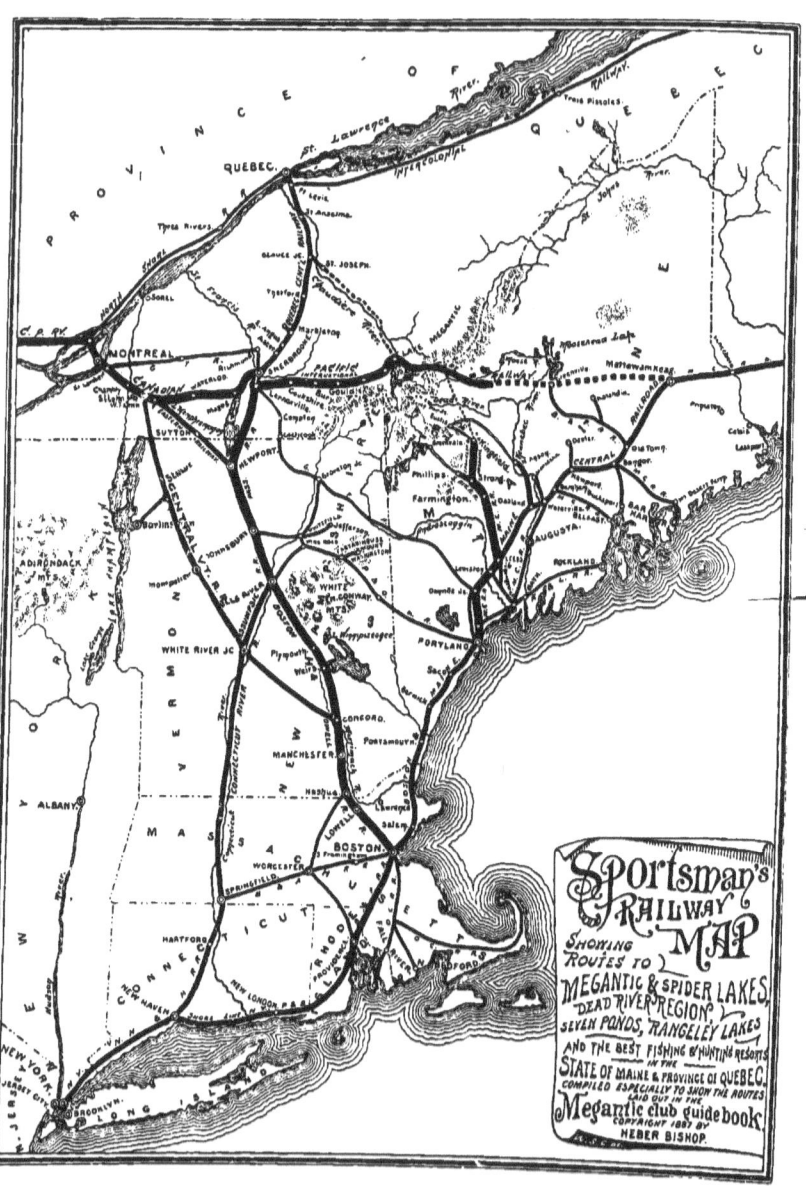

RETURNING

Leave Lake Megantic (International R'y) (Mondays, 7.45 A.M.)					5.30 A.M.
Arrive Sherbrooke	"	"	"	10.00 "	10.00 "
Leave Sherbrooke	(Passumpsic R.R.)				9.00 P.M.
Arrive Newport	"	"			10.45 "
Leave Newport	"	"			11.37 "
Arrive Wells River Junction	"	"			2.00 A.M.
" Springfield (Connecticut River R.R.)					7.10 "
Leave Springfield (N.Y., N.H. & H. R.R.)					7.30 "
Arrive New York	"	"	"	"	11.40 "

From Boston, one can take the route as follows: —

Leave Boston (Boston & Lowell R.R.)					7.00 P.M.
" Lowell	"	"	"		7.48 "
" Nashua (Concord R.R.)					8.20 "
" Manchester	"	"			8.54 "
" Concord (Boston & Lowell R.R.)					9.30 "
" Plymouth	"	"			11.40 "
" Wells River (Passumpsic R.R.)					2.00 A.M.
Arrive Newport	"	"			4.15 "
Leave Newport	"	"			6.00 "
Arrive Sherbrooke	"	"			7.45 "
Leave Sherbrooke (International R'y) (Saturdays, 3.30 P.M.)					3.00 P.M.
Arrive Lake Megantic	"	"	"	6.30 "	8.00 "

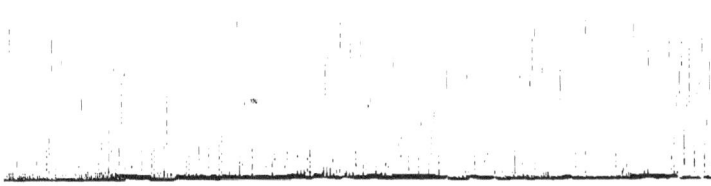

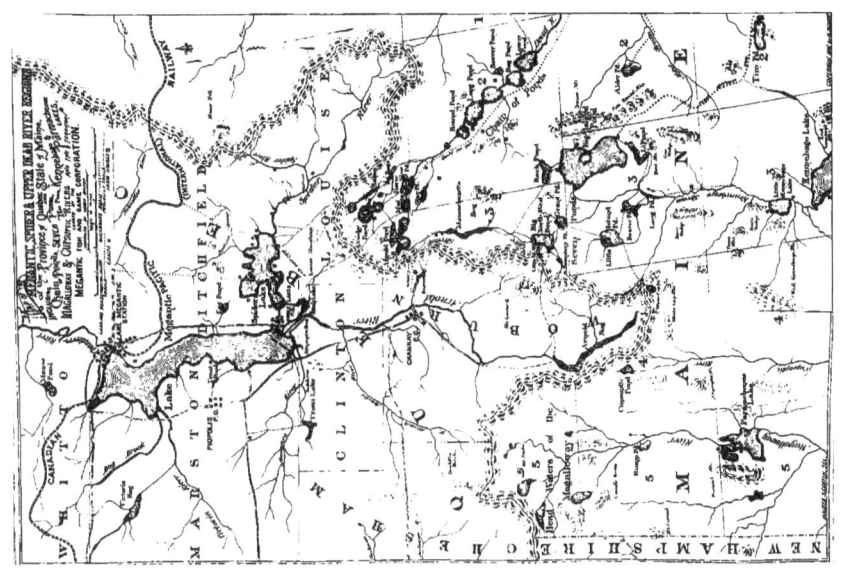

OWL'S HEAD MOUNTAIN. (Lake Memphremagog.)

RETURNING :—

Leave Lake Megantic (International R'y) (Mondays, 7.15 A.M.)				5.30 A.M.
Arrive Sherbrooke " " " 10.00 "				10.00 "
Leave Sherbrooke (Passumpsic R.R.)				9.00 P.M.
Arrive Newport " "				10.45 "
Leave Newport " "				11.37 "
" Wells River (Boston & Lowell R.R.)				2.00 A.M.
" Plymouth " " "				3.35 "
" Concord (Concord R.R.)				5.25 "
" Manchester " "				6.25 "
" Nashua (Boston & Lowell R.R.)				7.00 "
" Lowell " " "				7.35 "
Arrive Boston " " "				8.30 "

In returning from Lake Megantic, parties can reach Boston the same evening by telegraphing the mixed passenger train at Lennoxville to wait the arrival of the International at 9.45. The passenger is due to leave Lennoxville at 9.15, but being a mixed train will wait, when notified, for the International. This train arrives at Newport at 12.50 P.M., and connects with the day express from Montreal, leaving Newport at 1.03 P.M., and arriving at Boston at 8.35 P.M., saving just twelve hours' time, and making the trip from Spider Lake to Boston in sixteen hours.

The other route from Boston is by the Maine Central, *via* Farmington and Kingfield. The route this way is as follows : —

Leave Boston (Boston & Maine R.R., Eastern Division)	9.00 A.M.
Arrive Portland " " " " "	1.00 P.M.
Leave Portland (Maine Central R.R.)	1.25 "
Arrive Farmington " " "	5.50 "
Leave Farmington (Sandy River R.R.)	5.55 "
Arrive Strong " " "	6.40 "
Leave Strong (Franklin & Megantic R.R.)	6.45 "
Arrive Kingfield " " "	8.34 "
Leave Kingfield (Stage: Tuesdays, Thursdays, and Saturdays)	7.30 A.M.
Arrive Smith's Farm " " " " "	3.00 P.M.

Buckboard from Smith's farm to Seven Ponds, *via* Tim Pond.

RETURNING: —

Leave Smith's Farm, Eustis (Stage: Mondays, Wednesdays, and Fridays)	7.30 A.M.
Arrive Kingfield " " " " "	3.00 P.M.
Leave Kingfield (Franklin & Megantic R.R.)	5.35 A.M.
Arrive Strong " " "	7.25 "
Leave Strong (Sandy River R.R.)	7.30 "
Arrive Farmington " " "	8.15 "
Leave Farmington (Maine Central R.R.)	8.20 "
Arrive Portland " " "	12.40 P.M.
Leave Portland (Boston & Maine R.R.)	1.00 "
Arrive Boston " " "	5.00 "

WEIRS LANDING. (Lake Winnipesaukee.)

In point of time, Boston members effect a saving by going *via* the Boston & Lowell line. The express (Pullman attached) leaves the Lowell depot at 7 P.M., taking you through Lowell, Nashua, Manchester, Concord, Plymouth, past the beautiful Lake Winnipesaukee, which is reached about eleven o'clock, and on to Wells River, where the New York train is connected, and then over the Passumpsic to Newport, Vt., which is reached just at daybreak (4.15 A.M.), where a change of cars is necessary, as the Boston Pullman goes on to Montreal, the New York Pullman is switched off; and chairs can be obtained to Sherbrooke. While waiting to connect with the train for Sherbrooke, which leaves at six o'clock, one has time to look over the town, which is situated at the head of Lake Memphremagog. The large and well-patronized Memphremagog House shows what a popular and favorite summer resort this place is becoming; and one has a desire to remain over a day or two, or defer till the return trip, and spend a week in taking in the various places of interest in the locality, and enjoying the luxuries of the hotel. There is ample time for breakfast, if an early meal is desired. After leaving Newport, baggage is inspected by Her Majesty's customs officer. The law requires a deposit upon fire-arms taken across the boundary, but it is seldom enforced; and sportsmen to the Megantic region are always courteously treated by the officer, Mr. Clark, who passes all the paraphernalia required for going into camp, upon the understanding that they are personal effects, to be used

View on Lake Memphremagog (from Prospect Hill).

upon the trip, and not for sale. By the time the baggage is settled, the train arrives in sight of Massawippi Lake, which, although not so large as Memphremagog, rivals it in beauty; the train for miles winds along the border of the Lake, in places overhanging it, and affords passengers a charming view. After leaving the lake, the railway follows the course of the Massawippi River as far as Lennoxville, a very pretty village situated at the junction of the Massawippi and St. Francis Rivers. The trip from Lennoxville to Sherbrooke occupies less than ten minutes, where we arrive at 7.45 A.M.

Memphremagog House.

The town of Sherbrooke is situated upon a hill overlooking the Magog and St. Francis Rivers, which unite in about the center of the town. It contains nearly ten thousand inhabitants, and is the *chef-lieu* of the eastern townships. The train

SKETCH ON ST. FRANCIS RIVER, SHERBROOKE.

for Megantic does not leave till afternoon, which gives one time to look the city over at leisure. The city boasts of one of the largest tweed manufactories in Canada, good substantial public buildings, and fine private residences,— a drive through the residential portion of the city being very enjoyable. There are several fine Hotels, the largest, the Sherbrooke House, being situated immediately opposite the depot, where members will always be assured of a welcome from the genial proprietor, Mr. Coté, who is a veritable *rara avis* among hotel proprietors, and a member of the Club. While at Sherbrooke, either going or coming from the woods, members should not miss taking advantage of the very generous offer of the Quebec Central Railway to visit Quebec City, which is only about one hundred and twenty miles farther north. Club members will be given return tickets at single fare, making the cost of the trip less than four dollars.

Quebec City (from Point Levis).

THE ESPLANADE (DUFFERIN TERRACE), QUEBEC.

The journey from Sherbrooke to Quebec occupies only about six hours (palace cars are attached to all trains), and the scenery along the entire route is most romantic. The line follows the St. Francis Valley for the first thirty miles, then passes along the shores of Lake Aylmer and Black Lake, and through the famous asbestos mines of Thetford, till the Chaudière Valley is reached, with its rich rural parishes and gold fields. From here on to Point Levis, the tourist has an opportunity of observing the peculiar arrangement of French Canadian farms and villages, which contrast so strikingly with those of New England.

The train leaves Sherbrooke for Quebec at 8.15 A.M., arriving at Point Levis (opposite the city) at 2.20 P.M.; returning, leaves Levis at 2.45 P.M., arriving in Sherbrooke at 8.40 A.M. The tickets will be made good to stop over at Quebec for as long a time as desired. A proposed line is being laid out, extending up the Chaudière Valley from Beauce Junction via St. Joseph to Lake Megantic, connecting with the Canadian Pacific.

The train for Lake Megantic over the International Railway, a link of the Canadian Pacific, leaves Sherbrooke at 3 P.M. daily, arriving at the lake at 8 P.M.; but, on Saturdays, a fast train is put on, leaving half an hour later (3.30 P.M.), and arriving at the lake an hour and a half earlier (6.30 P.M.) On account of this arrangement, it is advisable to leave Boston on Friday evening, as by so doing one can reach Spider Lake the next evening before dark. The steamer "Lena" always connects with this train.

Upon any other day, if one wishes to proceed to the head of the lake the same evening, it will be necessary to telegraph Mr. George Flint, the proprietor of the steamer, to wait for the train, which he very kindly does for Club members without charge. Upon arriving at the lake, very comfortable quarters will be found at the Prince of Wales Hotel; and the proprietor, Mr. Moquin, will have all baggage taken from the depot to the steamer. The steamer " Lena " makes two regular trips daily (for time-table, see advertisement).

Until the Club House is ready, Three Lakes will be the objective point. A short carry of half a mile covers the distance to Spider Lake.

The other route from Boston is *via* the "Sportsman Line," — the Maine Central Railroad. This route is practically the shortest, but entails a few miles staging and buckboarding, which takes more time, but has the advantage of passing through a large territory noted for its fish and game attractions at all points. The train leaves the Eastern Division at 9 A.M., arriving in Portland at 1 P.M., where there is time for dinner. Leave Portland at 1.25 P.M., and at Leeds Junction change to the Farmington branch. From Leeds, the trip is up the Androscoggin River until Farmington is reached at 5.50 P.M. We now change to the Sandy River Railroad for Strong, where another change is necessary to the Franklin & Megantic Railroad, with its quaint little engines and coaches. The track is narrow gauge, the seats in the coaches having capacity for one person only. Despite the toy-like appearance of the train, very good time is made, and the present terminus at Kingfield reached at 8.34 P.M.

It is intended to push this road through *via* Eustis, to connect with the Canadian Pacific at or near Lake Megantic, which will make this route the best sportsman's line in the East.

The stage leaves at 7.30 next morning for Eustis, about twenty-five miles, arriving at Smith's farm at three o'clock in the afternoon, from which point buckboards are brought into requisition. Tim Pond, famous for its fishing, can be reached the same evening, the distance in being only seven miles.

A stop of a day or two here is very pleasant before taking the twelve mile journey to the Seven Ponds, at which point the Club trails begin leading to Lake Megantic.

Local Routes.

Having arrived at Three Lakes, over the Canadian Pacific Railway, the route in to the Chain of Ponds, or Seven Ponds, is as follows: Take the steamer across the lake to Woburn Wharf, where a carriage can be engaged to the foot of Beaver Bog, a distance of seven miles, over a good country road, one hour being the average time required. The charges for carriage hire for one or two persons with baggage (one horse) is $1.25, and for a double team $2.00. From the foot of Beaver Bog, for a distance of a mile, there is a ferry boat that will accommodate a large party, with baggage; and from the head of the bog to the boundary line (one mile) is a good buckboard road. A farmer, Mr. Gagné, whose house is situated at the boundary, will supply a horse at moderate rates. Arnold Pond is nearly a mile distant to the east from the farm, and Camp Massachusetts, at Massachusetts Bog, about two miles in a southerly direction. A road has been put through, so as to take a horse into the camp.

From Massachusetts Bog, the trails extend to the Seven Ponds, as laid down on the map; and one can make the round trip home, returning *via* Eustis or Kennebago and Rangeley Lakes. If so desired, take Kennedy Smith's buckboard road from Big Island Pond to Tim Pond, and from there to Eustis, and stage to Kingfield, the first railway point.

From the Seven Ponds, a number of fine trips can be taken in, and the camps owned by Mr. Viles at Big Island or Tim Pond, by Messrs. Grant and Richardson, of Kennebago Lake, visited, as well as Camp Caribou at Lake Parmachenee, kept by Mr. John Danforth; and, while at the Chain of Ponds, the

IMPORTANT NOTICE.

Just as the book was going to press arrangements were completed with the **Central Vermont Railroad** for special rates to Club members.

The rate for the round trip from Boston to Three Lakes (landing for Spider Lake), including steamer coupons, has been fixed at $14, and for New York members $18, making the cost of the trip about $3 less than by any other route.

The route *via* the Central Vermont is much more convenient in many respects than the Passumpsic, as Boston members can take the Pullman in Boston for St. Johns, P.Q., and not have to rise till 6.45 A.M., while by the Passumpsic route the Pullman has to be left at Newport at four o'clock in the morning; besides, members for an extra $2 can visit Montreal, which is only twenty-five miles off the route.

The trains leave Boston and New York at same stations and time as the route *via* Passumpsic, and arrives at Megantic at same time.

From Boston, take the 7 P.M. express (Boston & Lowell depot) Pullman *via* Central Vermont, which passes through Lowell, Nashua, leaving the Boston & Lowell Railroad at Concord, thence *via* White River Junction, Montpelier, and St. Albans, arriving at St. Johns, P.Q., at 6.45 A.M., where there is ample time to take breakfast at any of the hotels. At 8.30 A.M. the train, over the Northern Division Central Vermont Railroad, a link of the Canadian Pacific Railway, leaves for Sherbrooke, arriving at 11.55 A.M., in time for dinner. Take the Canadian Pacific (International) at 3 P.M. (Saturdays, 3.30 P.M.) for Lake Megantic, arriving at 8 P.M. (Saturdays, 6.30 P.M.)

New York members take the 4.30 P.M. express over the N.Y. N.H. & H. R.R. (Pullman at Springfield *via* Central Vermont) *via* New Haven, Hartford, Springfield, Brattleboro, Bellows Falls, Rutland, Burlington, and St. Albans, arriving at St. Johns at 6.45 A.M. (same time as Boston train). After breakfast leave at 8.30 A.M. for Sherbrooke and Lake Megantic.

Returning from Lake Megantic, leave at 5.30 A.M. (Mondays, 7.15 A.M.), arriving in Sherbrooke at 10 A.M. Leave Sherbrooke at 5.50 P.M. (instead of 9 P.M. *via* Passumpsic, and having a long wait at Newport), arriving at St. Johns at 9.20 P.M. Leave St. Johns (Pullman) 9.25 P.M., arriving in Boston at 8.30 A.M., or New York at 11.40 A.M.

The connections by this route, as will be seen, are good, and the long waits *via* the other routes avoided, and the Pullman accommodations are far superior, allowing members to get a Pullman earlier in the evening, and get up later in the morning. These advantages, together with the lowest rates given, will make this route the one to be patronized by the Club.

The tickets are to be had at Raymond's ticket office, 296 Washington Street, Boston. New York members will be supplied by E. R. Coppins, Passenger Agent Central Vermont Railroad, 317 Broadway, New York.

TIME TABLE, BOSTON TO LAKE MEGANTIC. (Central Vermont Route.)

```
Leave  Boston, Boston & Lowell R.R. . . . .  7.00 P.M.
  "    Lowell,      "      "      "   . . . .  7.48  "
  "    Nashua.   Concord R.R. . . . . . .    8.20  "
  "    Manchester,    "       "    . . . . .  8.54  "
  "    Concord. Northern R.R. . . . . . . .  9.30  "
Arrive St. Albans, Central Vermont R.R. . .  5.05 A.M.
  "    St. Johns,     "       "      "  . . .  6.45  "
Leave  St. Johns,     "       "      "  . . .  8.30  "
Arrive Sherbrooke,    "       "      "  . . . 11.55  "
Leave  Sherbrooke, International R'y (Satur-
         days, 3.30 P.M.) . . . . . . . . . .  3.00 P.M.
Arrive Megantic. International R'y (Saturdays,
         6.30 P.M.) . . . . . . . . . . . . .  8.00  "
```
This train has Pullman Buffet Sleeping Car from Boston to St. Johns, without change. Breakfast at hotel, St. Johns.

RETURNING : —
```
Leave  Megantic. International R'y (Mondays,
         7.15 A.M.) . . . . . . . . . . . . .  3.30 A.M.
Arrive Sherbrooke, International R'y (Mon-
         days. 10.00 A.M ) . . . . . . . . . 10.00  "
Leave  Sherbrooke. Central Vermont R.R. . .  5.30 P.M.
  "    St. Johns,     "       "      "  . . .  9.25  "
  "    St. Albans,    "       "      "  . . . 11.00  "
Arrive Concord, Northern R.R. . . . . . . .  5.50 A.M.
  "    Manchester, Concord R.R. . . . . . .  6.30  "
  "    Nashua,       "        "   . . . . . .  7.00  "
  "    Lowell, Boston & Lowell R.R. . . . .  7.35  "
  "    Boston,    "      "       "   . . . .  8.30  "
```
This train has Pullman Buffet Sleeping Car from St. Johns to Boston, without change.

TIME TABLE, NEW YORK TO LAKE MEGANTIC. (Central Vermont Route.)

```
Leave  New York. N.Y., N.H., & H. R.R. . .  4.30 P.M.
  "    New Haven,    "       "      "  . . .  6.26  "
  "    Hartford,     "       "      "  . . .  7.21  "
  "    Springfield. Connecticut River R.R. .  8.15  "
Arrive St. Albans. Central Vermont R.R. . .  5.05 A.M.
  "    St. Johns,    "       "      "  . . .  6.45  "
Leave  St. Johns,    "       "      "  . . .  8.30  "
Arrive Sherbrooke,   "       "      "  . . . 11.55  "
Leave  Sherbrooke. International R'y (Satur-
         days, 3.30 P.M.) . . . . . . . . . .  3.00 P.M.
Arrive Megantic, International R'y (Saturdays,
         6.30 P.M.) . . . . . . . . . . . . .  8.00  "
```
This train has Parlor Car New York to Springfield, and Pullman Palace Sleeping Car Springfield to St. Johns. Supper can be had on Dining Car between New Haven and Springfield, or at Springfield, and breakfast at hotel at St. Johns.

RETURNING : —
```
Leave  Megantic. International R'y (Mondays,
         7.15 A.M.) . . . . . . . . . . . . .  5.30 A.M.
Arrive Sherbrooke, International R'y (Mon-
         days. 10.00 A.M.) . . . . . . . . . 10.00  "
Leave  Sherbrooke. Central Vermont R.R. . .  5.50 P.M.
  "    St. Johns,    "       "      "  . . .  9.25  "
  "    St. Albans,   "       "      "  . . . 11.00  "
Arrive Springfield, Connecticut River R.R. .  7.10 A.M.
  "    Hartford,   N.Y., N.H., & H. R.R. . .  8.29  "
  "    New Haven,    "       "      "  . . .  9.35  "
  "    New York,     "       "      "  . . . 11.40  "
```
This train has Pullman Palace Sleeping Car from St. Johns to Springfield, and Parlor Car Springfield to New York. Breakfast at station dining rooms, Springfield.

trip to King and Bartlett Ponds, where Messrs. Douglas and St. Ober have camps, should be worth a trial. These places have been recently opened up for the accommodation of sportsmen, and offer many inducements to those fond of piercing back into the woods. If Hathan and Crosby Ponds are the desired places, they can be reached by the trail leading from Arnold Pond across to the outlet of Crosby Pond; but the nearest way to these two ponds is by trail direct to Spider Lake. The trail starts in at White Birch Camp, and the distance to Hathan Bog is five miles.

To reach Trout Lake, the carriage road from Lake Megantic (Mr. Ryan's farm) can be taken, and three miles of the distance driven to the farmhouse of Mr. Cusineau, where the trail for the lake (a little over two miles distant) commences. A considerable saving can be made by cutting a trail through direct from the Woburn Wharf, following the Clinton and Marston township line, which will probably be done another season.

FARES.

Since the passage of the Interstate Commerce Bill, the rates given the Club have been seriously interfered with, the promised rate of $9.50 from Boston (round trip), and $15 from New York, jumping up to $17 and $20.

So far, the Canadian Pacific Railway (which is not amenable to the law) is the only railway that has offered us special rates. It makes the round trip from Sherbrooke or Lennoxville to Spider Lake and return (including coupons for steamer on Lake Megantic) $2.35 to Club members; from Cookshire, $1.85. These tickets are procured upon presentation of a certificate of membership, or a requisition signed by the Club Secretary. The regular return fare from Boston to Sherbrooke is $14, making the round trip ticket $16.35.

These tickets, containing the Canadian Pacific and steamer coupons, can be obtained at Raymond's ticket office, 296 Washington Street, Boston.

Boston members can, by purchasing mileage tickets (Boston & Lowell Railroad) good between Boston and Sherbrooke, bring the fare down to less than $14.

It is expected that better rates can be made over this route; but, on account of the new deals between the Passumpsic, Boston & Lowell, and Boston & Maine Railroads, and present unsettled condition, nothing can be accomplished for the coming season.

New York members can get tickets to Lake Megantic (not including steamer coupons) for $20 the round trip, or purchase tickets from New York to Sherbrooke and return, and at Sherbrooke get the Club tickets for the round trip to Spider Lake. A special rate over the Canadian Pacific Railway will be given Toronto and Montreal members to Spider Lake and return. The fare over the Maine Central is much cheaper, being only $13.50 for the round trip from Boston to Eustis (Smith's farm). From this point, if buckboards are employed, the rate is $5 from Eustis to Tim Pond, and $12.50 to the Seven Ponds (each way) for the buckboard, which will, however, accommodate more than one passenger.

GUIDES.

As regards GUIDES, if members will write to the Club fish and game overseer, Mr. W. E. Latty, whose address is Post-office, Three Lakes, P.Q., he will secure guides. Among those at Lake Megantic are Peter Matheson, one of the Club game wardens during the close season, but who will guide between October 1 and January 1; Kenneth McRae, post-office address, Winslow, P.Q.; Russell Edwards and George Bachelder, Lake Megantic, P.Q.; Elijah Mills, Francis Mills, and Peter LeRoyer (Indian),

Three Lakes, P.Q. Martin Fuller (Smith's Farm, Stratton, Me.) will guide members, and is thoroughly acquainted with the Seven Ponds region, Tim Pond, and Kennebago Lakes, as well as the Megantic region.

The following guides are thoroughly acquainted with the entire Dead River region, and can be engaged by addressing them; many of them have also guided about the Megantic and Spider Lakes: Grant Fuller, Robert Phillips, Stratton, Me.; John Sylvester, William Sylvester, William Lockier, John Day, Alexander Dutelley, Eustis, Me.; Henry Dill, David Haynes, Elmer Snowman, Jean Soule, William Haynes, Dexter Huntoon, Warren Stevens, Stephen Lowell, Rufus Porter, and Warren Wilbur, Rangeley, Me.

The following well-known guides are proprietors of camps, and have every facility for the accommodation of sportsmen: A. S. Douglas and Joe St. Ober, at King and Bartlett Ponds; Edgar Smith, manager at Viles' camps, Big Island Pond; Thomas Cross, manager at Viles' camps, at Tim Pond; John Danforth, at Camp Caribou, Lake Parmachenee; Grant and Richardson, at Lake Kennebago (Kennebago House); Walter Twombly and Rufus Crosby, at Rangeley Lakes (Mooselucmaguntic House); and Jean Soule, in charge of Mason's camp, Big Island Pond.

Members wishing to engage the services of any of the Eustis or Rangeley guides can do so, and by appointment be met at Lake Megantic. Those guides owning camps, as a rule, will only guide their guests, and in the region about the camps, but can furnish guides for going back into the woods. The universal terms for guides are $2.00 per day and board, which includes use of boats.

MEGANTIC FISH AND GAME CORPORATION.

PROSPECTUS.

Boston, December 1, 1886.

Dear Sir :—

An eminent writer has said. "It becomes the duty of every sportsman, when he discovers a new El Dorado, to make known his good fortune to others of like tastes, provided there be room in the newly found region for all who may come."

This may be taken as my apology, if such be needed, for addressing you concerning a territory which, though not wholly unknown, is comparatively new to most lovers of hunting and fishing, and which possesses such a wealth of attractions that it is eminently worthy of careful investigation.

This territory of over forty thousand acres lies mainly in the eastern part of the Province of Quebec, but extends into Maine, containing a great number of lakes and ponds, and immense stretches of forests. During a residence of two years at Lake Megantic, and several vacation seasons since spent in that region, I have had ample opportunity to become thoroughly acquainted with all the ponds and streams in the vicinity of Megantic and Spider Lakes, as well as the adjoining headwaters of the Dead River in Maine, and have often been greatly surprised at the wonderful abundance of fish and game in every direction.

While participating with friends in the rare sport thus afforded, it was suggested that a society ought to be formed for the protection of the fish and game of that region. The matter was frequently and fully discussed, and, becoming convinced that there would be no lack of support from gentlemen who were fond of good hunting and fishing, I approached the Quebec Government and the private landowners in Maine, for the purpose of leasing the desired territory, so that it might be controlled and kept stocked and protected.

In this new enterprise, I received sufficient encouragement to warrant the formation of a *Fish and Game Club*. Arrangements have been made with the Crown Lands Department at Quebec for a lease of the Spider River and its tributaries, with other waters in the vicinity, also Arnold Bog and all that portion of the Arnold River belonging to the Crown. These leases, together with some private leases of the Lower Spider River, Rush Lake, and the eastern shore of Spider Lake, will give the Club complete control of the best fishing waters on the Canadian side of the boundary, while similar arrangements with private landholders in the contiguous part of Maine will control the headwaters of the Dead River region, comprising lakes and ponds teeming with speckled trout, and already noted for the certainty of good fishing at any time of the season.

Speckled trout abound in the Spider River, Arnold River, Rush Lake, and Lake Megantic; black bass in Spider Lake; land-locked salmon in the Upper Arnold River and Arnold Bog; lake trout or "lunge" in Lake Megantic; and speckled trout and lunge in the Dead River lakes. In the last season (1886), a lake trout weighing *twenty pounds* was caught in Lake Megantic, and a speckled trout (genuine *Salmo fontinalis*) weighing seven pounds was taken in the Spider River.

The Upper Spider River is one of the most prolific trout streams in the Province. Two friends caught in this stream, with flies, in the month of June, in less than two hours, seventy-four trout, weighing in the aggregate seventy-five pounds, six of the largest averaging four and one-half pounds each; also, three gentlemen, in a forenoon's fishing, caught in this stream two hundred and fifty-two trout in August, 1885. The fishing in Lake Megantic, although good at times, is very uncertain, the most propitious months being May, June, and September. Fabulous stories have been told of the size and number of fish caught in this lake at different times, the following well authenticated catch occurring under my own observation: A lady, in a September's afternoon of 1882, caught, off Rocky Point, thirteen trout, aggregating fifty-four pounds, the largest one weighing six and one-quarter pounds.

In speaking of the black-bass fishing in Spider Lake, a correspondent of the Sherbrooke *Examiner* writes: "This lake affords good bass fishing with bait, spoon, or fly; and, with adequate protection, this sport could be considerably increased. Two of us have taken with spoon, in two hours, twenty-eight bass, averaging three pounds each."

The game supply in this territory cannot be surpassed, and it is expected that the co-operation with the Club of the authorities of the Province of Quebec and Maine will result in the protection and perpetuation of one of the most valuable large game resorts on the eastern portion of this continent.

Owing to the situation and formation of the land, this locality is peculiarly adapted to the breeding of moose, caribou, and deer. From the Spider River, through to the Seven Ponds and Magalloway River, there is one dense forest, interspersed with mountains, small lakes, and bogs. Large tracts of land bordering upon the waters have been completely burned over, destroying the lumber, and leaving granite ledges exposed, with only soil enough to grow the weeds and low shrubbery which large game feed upon. As the land can never become arable, there is no danger that the game will ever be driven out by the advance of civilization. The situation is upon the watershed dividing the waters which flow into the St. Lawrence from the headwaters of the Androscoggin, Magalloway, and Kennebec Rivers in Maine, about twenty miles from Eustis, Me., and eighty miles easterly from Sherbrooke, P.Q. The elevation is nearly three thousand feet above the sea level, rendering it a most healthful summer resort, especially for persons with weak lungs. It is distant four miles from Seven Ponds, twelve from Lake Parmachenee, three from the Chain of Ponds, and a short distance by rail from the Moose River region, recently opened up by the construction of the International Railway.

In the section to be protected by the Club, the usual lawlessness, from habit, has long existed, and it is only recently that the inhabitants upon the border have begun to be aware of the efficacy of game laws. As an illustration of the wanton and wholesale slaughter indulged in heretofore,—also showing. incidentally, the abundance of game,— let me cite a well authenticated case: In this region, in the winter of 1869-70, two hunters, a white and an Indian, killed two hundred and sixty-five moose between January 15 and April 15, taking only their skins. An old hunter told me last summer, with an air of pride, that fifteen years ago last June he killed in one night, in Rush Lake (now leased to the Club), five moose, three of which were cows. Indeed, it is not necessary to go so far back to find instances showing the abundance of game here and the necessity of protection. Only two years ago last April, two French Canadians killed, on premises now leased to our Club, six moose in one week, four of which were cows then with calf; and only a year ago last June another French Canadian killed two moose in one night, in a small bog off the

Arnold River. [The law forbids the taking of moose or deer between February 1 and September 1, and prohibits the taking of *female* moose at any time until after October 15, 1888.]

Probably the most atrocious recent violation of game laws was the slaughter, by " still-hunting " and hounds, of hundreds of deer, of which 2,700 pounds of *hind-quarters only* were shipped to the Boston market, *via* Kingfield, Me., in April of last year. The fore-quarters were left in the woods. These deer were all killed (the greater number in Maine) on the territory now leased to our Club, and within six miles of the proposed Club House. It has heretofore been a difficult matter to protect game along either side of the international boundary, although the game wardens of Franklin County, Me., and the Provincial bush ranger, Mr. Parker Nagle, have accomplished much good. But the need of an International Fish and Game Club, in active co-operation with the Provincial and Maine authorities, is very apparent. The following extracts from the annual report of the Fish and Game Commissioners of Maine, just published, will help to show the needs of the case:—

" The boundaries of one-half of the State over which we are expected to extend our protection and care are upon the Dominion of Canada. Canadian citizens and Indians kill our game in close time, crust-hunt our moose, break all our laws with impunity, and escape beyond the reach of our authority. This is why we require a good and efficient guard upon the boundaries. . . . Our game laws are fair and impartial to all. They only seek to protect the game when it is breeding, or when nursing its young, or when recuperating after the season is passed. It is merely sought to insure to the workingman, whether at manual labor, or at the desk, or factory, or sawmill, an equal right to his share of what belongs equally to all. . . . We require a square non-exportation law. There are enough deer for all, and the law has made a fair apportionment of three to each. One moose, two caribou, and three deer is the apportionment made by our Legislature for each man. . . . Many moose have, doubtless, migrated into our State from other forests, but there has been a very marked increase in their numbers in our own woods. Notwithstanding this one favorable feature, we fear their early and utter extermination, unless the Legislature will give us both money for enforcement, and laws to control. The slaughter of moose of all ages and sexes the last two years, by crust-hunting poachers, has been most pitiful. Thirteen moose-hides taken last spring by one Indian guide were lately found in his possession."

Concerning the moose, the commissioners say: " The high market value of the moose skin is as great a temptation to the idle vagabond poacher as is a well filled safe to his brother scoundrel, the professional cracksman. Many of the guides, some of whom are Indian, after earning good wages from their employers, and after the season is over, seek out the wintering yards of the moose, and in the snow crust of spring slaughter all, even down to the worthless calf. If the yard is handy to a winter camp of lumbermen, the meat is sold; if far away, they are killed for the skins alone. The whites and Indians, both of our own or neighboring scoundrels, are engaged in this destruction of our moose. The few bulls killed by our visiting sportsmen would never exterminate the race, for rarely is a cow moose killed, as they do not come to the call of the hunter. It is the destruction of the cows by the crust-hunter that is to lead to their utter extermination, if not summarily stopped by the enforcement of severe laws."

There are not less than fifty deer killed annually at Spider and Rush Lakes alone, not including those captured in the deep snow. In paddling up the Spider River, three miles and return, I have often seen six to eight deer feeding upon the banks. Seven deer and one moose were seen the same afternoon and evening, in going from Spider Lake to the lower end of Hathan Bog in Maine, a distance of five miles. Upon an average, six moose are killed every year in Spider River and vicinity (last year, I personally knew of five, and this season, so far, six), besides what are taken in deep snow by "crust-hunters."

The Canadian partridge and ruffled grouse abound throughout the territory, and afford fine sport in the fall months. Wild ducks are in great abundance during the migratory period, and a considerable number breed in the region. This latter number could be greatly increased by sowing wild rice about the shores of the lakes, as at the present time there is not much for ducks to feed on.

It is intended to build, at Spider Lake, a large Club House, containing forty or fifty rooms. A small steam launch, now in construction, will be placed upon Spider Lake for the use of members of the Club, and will connect with the steamer on Lake Megantic. Hunting and fishing boats will also be placed upon Spider Lake and River, and canoes and boats in the other streams and waters. An overseer has been appointed who will give his entire time to the protection of fish and game, and who will receive appointments from the Dominion and Provincial Governments, as well as aid from the Maine Commission. Four assistant wardens will be appointed to assist the overseer at certain seasons when lawlessness is most prevalent,—*e.g.*, during the crust-hunting season in February, March, and April; at such times, the wardens will systematically patrol the region in search of poachers. Again in June, July, and August, their services will be brought into requisition to prevent the killing of deer by "jack-shooting," and a warden will be camped at each group of ponds where that is now practiced. During the open season for hunting and fishing, these wardens will be engaged in the prevention of unlawful fishing, netting, etc. Through such endeavors, and under such protection, the fish and game must rapidly increase. It is estimated that, at the present time, the number of deer killed in and out of season, in this region, does not equal the annual increase. What an amount of legitimate sport may be expected, when these are properly protected, may be imagined.

The Club will, from time to time, as may be found needful, restock the waters with trout and land-locked salmon, although, with fair care and protection. the fishing will be good for many years to come, and only two or three of the lakes and streams will require immediate replenishing.

On account of the facilities for obtaining supplies, the members of the Club can be boarded in the Club House at the low rate of $5.00 per week, or $1.00 per day, and at the latter rate in the various camps. The Club House will be under the management of a competent and experienced man, with housekeeper and servants, while the camps will be fully equipped, and be in charge of the various guides.

Lake Megantic is reached from Boston *via* Boston & Lowell R.R., Concord, Lake Winnipesaukee, Plymouth, Wells River, and Newport, Vt., to Sherbrooke, P.Q.; thence by International R.R. to Lake Megantic, steamer to Three Lakes, and a carry of half a mile covers the distance to Spider Lake. From New York *via* N. Y., N. H. & H. R.R. to Springfield; Conn. River R.R. to Wells River Junction; Passumpsic R.R. over same route *via* Sherbrooke. From New York, take 4.30 P.M. train, in Pullman, to Sherbrooke, connecting with Boston train at Wells River. The latter leaves Boston (B. & L.) at 7 P.M., with Pullman to Newport, Vt., arriving at Spider Lake before noon next day; returning, leaves Spider Lake at 5 A.M., reaching Boston at 8.30 P.M. same day.

Through the kind courtesy of Mr. W. Raymond, General Agent of the Montreal & Boston Air Line, and Mr. N. P. Lovering, General Ticket Agent Passumpsic R.R., Lyndonville, Vt., members of the Club will be furnished with tickets (unlimited). Boston to Megantic and return, at the extremely low rate of $9.50, or $10 to Spider Lake, including coupons for steamer on Lake Megantic; from White River Junction, round trip, $5.00; from New York, round trip to Spider Lake, including coupons for steamer, $15. Mr. McFee, Superintendent of International R.R., kindly puts rates for Sherbrooke and Lennoxville members at $2.00 for round trip. Correspondingly low rates are being arranged for Quebec and Montreal members. These special rates will be given to Club members only, upon presentation of a requisition signed by the Secretary of the Club.*

* Since the passage of the Interstate Commerce Bill, these rates have been canceled.

It will thus be seen that lovers of the rod and gun visiting this region will, by becoming members of the Megantic Club, more than save their Club dues by the reduction in traveling charges, as well as securing all the advantages of the Club in materially reducing all other expenses.

The Club will be incorporated under the laws of the Province of Quebec and State of Maine.

The membership was at first limited to one hundred, but, that limit being nearly reached in a short time, it was deemed advisable to extend the limit to one hundred and fifty, with $50 initiation fee and $10 annual dues, or to go farther and make it three hundred members, with $25 fee and $5 annual dues.*

It was suggested that, if the latter be adopted, many friends of game protection in the vicinity of this region would join and pay dues annually, for the purpose alone of carrying on the good work; and it is not the intention of the Club to exclude reputable sportsmen by fixing a high admission fee. These questions of limitation and fees will be decided at the annual meeting, to be held at the Parker House, in Boston, January 11, 1887. Intending members should at once apply to the provisional Secretary for application forms, sending them in return before the above date, and stating their views upon the subject, if they wish to have a voice in the determination of these important questions. It is important that as many members as possible may be registered before that time, in order that certain improvements may be decided upon at that meeting, and that our game wardens may be put at work before the commencement of the close season for deer and moose, which will soon be at hand.

The admission fees can only be used for improvements, such as building the Club House, camps, boats, trails, and furnishings. The cost of protecting fish and game, continuing the leases, repairing buildings, boats, etc., together with all running expenses, must be paid from the annual dues, every dollar of initiation fees going to provide permanent improvements for the comfort of the members.

At the annual meeting in January, the Constitution, By-Laws, Rules and Regulations will be adopted, the *personnel* of the Club elected, fish and game wardens appointed and confirmed, and all the general work of the Club be put in motion. By that time, all the leases will be complete; and after the meeting a *Club Guide Book* will be

* Finally incorporated with a capital of $25,000, divided into five hundred shares at $50 each, one share necessary for membership, and the annual dues not to exceed $10 in any one year.

issued at the earliest practicable day, containing the Constitution, By-Laws, Rules and Regulations, a digest of the Provincial and Maine laws concerning fish and game, full information concerning all the lands and waters leased, and illustrated with maps and photo-engravings. It will also give ample information regarding the entire territory, routes, railway fares, etc.,—being made a complete and reliable guide.

It is not expected that the Club House can be ready before the summer months; but, pending its erection, the provisional Secretary will be pleased to place his summer house at Spider Lake, with its equipments, boats, etc., at the disposal of members; and it is confidently hoped that the Club House will be ready for occupancy by the opening of the September shooting season, or earlier.

Blank applications for membership, with copies of Constitution and By-Laws, will be mailed to any person desiring to become a member, on application.

Trusting that the enterprise may receive the patronage its merits deserve, and that you may become interested therein, I am,

                                        Very truly yours,

Hoffman House, Boston.   HEBER BISHOP.

PROVINCE OF QUEBEC, CANADA, CHARTER.

Granted under the provisions of the Act 48 Vict., chap. 12, entitled "An Act to facilitate the formation of fish and game protection clubs in the Province."

By virtue of an order in Council No. 138, approved by His Honor the Lieutenant Governor of the Province of Quebec on the twenty-sixth day of March, 1887, Dr. Heber Bishop, of Boston; Col. Gustavus Lucke, of Sherbrooke; Major W. A. Morehouse, G. H. Gordon, Francis P. Buck, of Sherbrooke; Ubert K. Pettingill, George C. Ainsworth, Erastus Willard, Fred A. Cooke, Col. Samuel Harrington, Jacob P. Bates, James N. Frye, all of Boston, Mass.; Isaac O. Woodruff, Henry W. Nason, John W. Mason, F. H. Southwick, all of the city of New York; Hon. Henry Aylmer, of

Richmond ; Alexander Ross, of Gould ; Rufus H. Pope, of Cookshire ; Chs. W. Hinman, of Roslindale, Mass. ; Chs. S. Hanks, of Cambridge, U. S. A. ; Chs. P. Hazeltine, of Belfast, Maine ; and all other persons who are now or who may hereafter become members of the Club, incorporated in virtue of the said order in Council, are hereby constituted a body corporate and politic under the name of " Megantic Fish and Game Club of the Province of Quebec."

The capital stock of the said company is twenty-five thousand dollars, divided into five hundred shares of fifty dollars each ; and its aim and end is to aid in the enforcement of the laws and regulations for the protection of fish and game in the Province, and for the other objects mentioned in the said act.

DEPARTMENT OF CROWN LANDS,
QUEBEC, 29 March, 1887.

E. E. TACHE,
Asst. Commissioner, Crown Lands.

INCORPORATED UNDER THE LAWS OF THE

STATE OF MAINE,

FEBRUARY 18th, 1887.

OBJECTS OF THE CLUB.

The objects of the Club are: the enforcement of the Fishery and Game Laws; the preservation, propagation, and breeding of fish and game; and the hiring, leasing, and purchasing of lands and waters, in order to furnish facilities to members for hunting, shooting, and fishing.

The first meeting for organizing the Club was held in Boston in January last; and, as a result, a Corporation was formed under the laws of the State of Maine, in Portland, on February 18, 1887, and officers and directors elected for the ensuing year. The charter in the Province of Quebec was granted on March 26, 1887, the capital stock of the Corporation being fixed at $25,000, divided into five hundred shares at $50 each. Since incorporation, meetings of the Board of Directors have been held as often as once a month, and the general machinery of the Club set in motion.

Two game wardens have been appointed on the Canadian side of the boundary, and commissioned by the Quebec Government (and lately as fish guardians also), and one warden in the State of Maine. These wardens are employed continuously, their salaries being paid monthly; and it is their duty to see that no game or fish is taken out of season in the district, and to prevent poaching upon the Club preserves.

The most desirable waters in the region have been leased, the leases running from five to ten years, with the privilege of extension,— the leased territory extending from Spider and Megantic Lakes as far south as (and including some of) the Seven Ponds in Maine.

The Crown Lands Department of the Province of Quebec have leased to the Club the exclusive fishing rights of all the inland waters in the township of Louise (20,571 acres), which include the Spider River, and also, in the unsubdivided portion of the township of Woburn, 10,811 acres, which include the headwaters of the Arnold River and Arnold Bog. Leases made with private landholders in the Province include over two thousand acres fronting

THE PROPOSED CLUB HOUSE. (From the Architect's Plans.)

upon Spider Lake (the whole southern shore), Lower Spider River, Rush Lake, and the head of Lake Megantic. In Maine, the leases are made with the owners of townships. The whole territory covered by the Club's leases will include over seventy-five thousand acres, or one hundred and twenty square miles.

At the present time, it is impossible to lay down the exact limits of the territory, as negotiations for leases are still in process of completion; but, by the time of the next issue of this book, it will be possible to print in color upon the map the Club preserves, showing the exact boundaries. Besides the leases, the Corporation has lately purchased a considerable tract of land in the township of Ditchfield, lying between Spider Lake and the township of Louise.

The improvements as laid out in the prospectus are being pushed ahead, the only drawback has been in the selection of a location for the Club House, which has prevented this portion of the programme from being carried out. Early this spring, plans were made and submitted to the Board, and duly accepted. Tenders were asked for, and the contract all but awarded, with the full expectation of having the Club House completed by the opening of the shooting season, when difficulties arose regarding the site, and, on account of the deep snow, the choice of the location was deferred till the ice went out. At the stockholders' annual meeting, held in Portland in May, it was decided to award the contract as soon as the site was fixed upon, and a committee was chosen to negotiate for the land. The committee visited Spider Lake a week or two after the ice went out, and their choice lay between one of two locations; but the land was held at such an exorbitant figure, the committee did not feel disposed to recommend the purchase, and, a question having arisen concerning the title, matters are still pending, with the chances in favor of delaying the erection of the building until too late for occupancy the present season.

When the first chapter of this book was written, it was fully expected the Club House would be ready by the time the book was out; and it is to be hoped that the arrangements will soon be completed, and the work go on. The plans as accepted provided for a building one hundred feet long, including the piazzas; the body of the house seventy-six by thirty-two feet; three stories and an attic; the first floor divided into a spacious dining-room, hall, reading-room, billiard hall, and cloak room, with large, open, old-fashioned stone fireplaces in the dining-room, hall, and reading-room; the second and third floors divided into twenty-four bedrooms, ten by twelve feet, — the kitchen, storerooms, and apartments for employees being in a separate building.

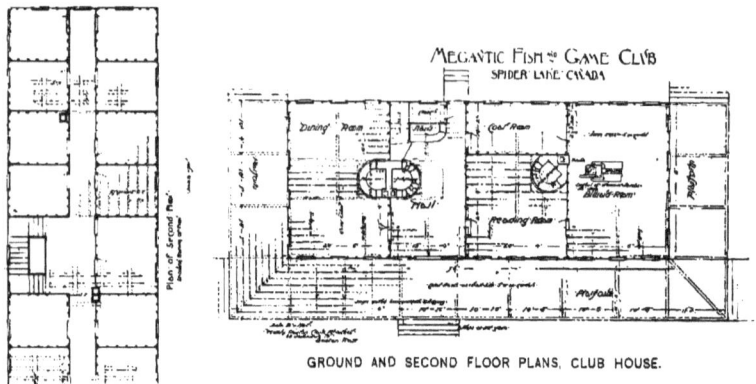

GROUND AND SECOND FLOOR PLANS, CLUB HOUSE.

Pending the erection of the Club House, a superintendent has been engaged, who with a crew of men has commenced the erection of several of the Club camps and trails. This work is steadily advancing, and good accommodations will be found at many of the ponds. The trails have been surveyed in the most practical places, and cut through in some instances wide enough to take in a horse with supplies; the camps are furnished with stoves, cooking utensils, dishes, and blankets; and boats are being built to place upon the ponds.

The hull for the Club steamer, to ply upon Spider Lake, will be completed by the first of August, and the engine

The Club Steamer.

(already built) will be taken out and put in the boat by the middle of the month. The engine was built by the Shipman Engine Company, of Boston; is automatic in its supply, and uses kerosene oil for fuel,— a low grade of oil worth in Boston seven cents per gallon,— and when running at full speed will consume not more than half a gallon per hour. No skilled engineer is required, as the entire engine is automatic; it is only necessary that the engine receives a constant supply of oil and water, and any of the Club guides or wardens can run it. There is no dirt or smoke, and the boat is not encumbered with wood or coal, the oil being stored in a tank under the stern or bow. The engine and boiler occupy a space of twenty-four by thirty inches in the center of the boat, the boat being twenty-two feet long, four and a half foot beam, with a seating capacity of twelve to fifteen persons,— estimated speed, six to eight miles per hour.

The facilities for still-hunting in the fall of the year, in the reservation in Maine particularly, are very good, the best time being upon the first snow, which is generally late in November or in December.

The entire Club territory is a most prolific one, as regards large game and trout, the greater portion of it being situated along the international boundary, and is already well stocked with moose, caribou, and deer, while nearly all the waters, which include twenty-four ponds and four rivers, will not require restocking for some time to come. The Club will not accept over three hundred members for the first year or two of its existence, at least, and, by limiting the amount of fish and game to be taken by each visiting member, hopes to establish and perpetuate a preserve that will be unequaled anywhere upon the eastern section of the continent.

Very important changes have lately been made in the Quebec game laws. Heretofore, the open season for deer and moose commenced on September 1 and closed February 1, which gave a long hunting season, and allowed one to combine fishing and hunting during the month of September. In May last (1887), the Quebec Legislature amended the laws and shortened the season two months, closing the months of September and January. The closing of the month of January was a most wise proceeding, as the slaughter of deer during that month the last season, on account of the deep snow, was appalling, and as a result deer will increase at least twenty-five per cent. more; but shutting off the month of September was a great disappointment to many, and, although needed along the Ottawa River and north shore of the St. Lawrence, it was totally unnecessary in the eastern portion of the Province of Quebec, where deer are so plentiful. While, as a matter of course, the deer will greatly increase, it puts a premium upon poaching, and the average inhabitant is practically shut out from killing deer at all, for the settler who is not a practical sportsman cannot still-hunt a deer; and from October to January it is well-nigh impossible to take them in any other manner. Presumably, the reason for making September a close month is to allow the deer to recuperate after rearing their young; but, in a territory where deer are so plentiful, such legislation is unnecessary. The ordinary sportsman will not shoot a doe in September, as they are not fit to eat, while the bucks are in excellent condition; and the thinning out of a few of them in September, when they can be hunted in the vicinity of the waters and with comparative ease, is not deleterious to the propagation of the species.

The professional or business man cannot as a rule remain in the woods after October, as the requirements of business demand his return to the city; but he can generally get a fortnight as late as September, when he may expect fair success at fishing, and the pleasure of deer hunting ought not to be denied him.

For the past three years, the Quebec Legislature has prohibited the taking of female moose at any time. Why not make the same law apply to does, or during the month of September, making the month open for bucks? In Maine, the best protected State in the Union, the repeal of the law making September a close month was nearly passed last winter, and public sentiment is fast leaning in that direction,— that the law in September is *now* unnecessary. Very bitter complaints are made by both sportsmen and settlers in the eastern portion of Quebec, and during the next parliament a memorial will be presented on behalf of making September an open month.

At the same time the amendment to the game laws in Quebec was passed, a most judicious measure was adopted, prohibiting the taking of moose (male or female) *at any time* previous to October, 1890. The moose is becoming extinct fast enough, the territory now included in the Club preserve along the international boundary being almost the last resort of these noble animals in that section of the country; and, although within the last two years moose have become a little more numerous, this law will be the means, if properly enforced, of giving the moose a chance to predominate in the region once more. Since the appointment of the Club game wardens, the very encouraging reports have come in that "so far not a single moose has been killed since the close season commenced," although in former years they were killed by the score every season by crust-hunters.

The Club Directors have authority to make their own fish and game laws governing members upon the Club territory, and it is expected that not only the State and Provincial laws, but the Club rules will be thoroughly observed and enforced by all its members.

BY-LAWS.

ARTICLE I.
ORGANIZATION.

This Corporation shall be known as the Megantic Fish and Game Corporation.

ARTICLE II.
PURPOSES OF ORGANIZATION.

The object of this Corporation is the propagation of fish and game.

ARTICLE III.
MEETINGS OF THE STOCKHOLDERS.

The Annual Meeting of the Stockholders shall be held on the second Tuesday of May, at Portland, in the State of Maine, for the transaction of any legal business of the Corporation. Not less than fourteen days' previous notice of the time and place of holding said meeting shall be given by the Clerk or Assistant Clerk, by mailing a notice thereof to each stockholder, at his post-office address, as of record on the books of the Corporation.

Three stockholders shall be requisite to constitute a quorum for the transaction of any business. In the absence of a quorum, the meeting shall be adjourned.

Representation of one-fourth of the capital stock shall be necessary for the transaction of any business at the stockholders' meetings.

At all meetings of the stockholders, each share of stock shall be entitled to one vote, and said vote shall be cast by the holder, in person or by proxy, within the limitations now or hereafter provided by law.

On any question, a stock vote shall be taken upon the demand of any stockholder.

ARTICLE IV.

OFFICERS.

The officers of the Corporation shall be a President, two Vice-Presidents, a Treasurer, a Clerk of Corporation, an Assistant Clerk of Corporation, who may be appointed Corresponding Secretary, and a Board of twenty-six Directors.

ARTICLE V.

THE PRESIDENT.

The President shall preside at all meetings of the Board of Directors and stockholders, and shall be entitled to vote on all questions.

He may call special meetings of the Board of Directors at his discretion, four days' written notice being given, and shall call such meetings when requested in writing by two of the Board.

He shall call special meetings of the stockholders, when so requested in writing by a majority of the Board of Directors, or upon request in writing of the stockholders representing one-fourth of the capital stock, fourteen days' written notice of the same being given to each stockholder.

He shall sign, as President, all certificates of stock and all contracts and other instruments which it is necessary to have in writing, and which have first been approved by the Board of Directors.

He shall prepare, in time to lay before the stockholders at their annual meeting, or oftener if required, an accurate account of the operations of the Corporation, during the time succeeding his last report, and also a statement of the

property and resources of the Corporation, its funded and floating debt, if any, outstanding accounts, and contingent liabilities, etc.
He shall perform such other duties as are prescribed by law, or may be prescribed by the Board of Directors.

ARTICLE VI.
THE VICE-PRESIDENT.

The Vice-President shall preside at all meetings of the Directors or stockholders in the absence of the President.
He shall call special meetings of the Board of Directors, upon the written request of two of the Board, four days' written notice having been given the members of the Board of the same.

ARTICLE VII.
THE TREASURER.

It shall be the duty of the Treasurer to receive all moneys of the Corporation, and deposit the same in some bank, to be designated by the Board of Directors.
He shall disburse the same under the direction of the Board, upon an order countersigned by three of its members.
He shall, at the Annual Meeting of the Stockholders, submit a complete statement of his accounts for the past year with the proper vouchers, together with a correct inventory of the property and effects of the Corporation.
He shall give a bond for the faithful discharge of his duties, in such sum and with such sureties as the Board of Directors shall require.
He shall, in the manner prescribed by the Board of Directors, keep proper books of account, a stock ledger, and a transfer book, showing the residence and post-office address of all the stockholders, and number of shares issued to, and transferred by, any stockholder, and the date of such issuance and transfer.
It shall be his duty to make up an account of the pecuniary condition of the Corporation, whenever required by the President or Directors so to do.
He shall have charge of the Corporate Seal, and affix the same to all instruments requiring a seal.
He shall sign, as Treasurer, all certificates of stock.
He shall discharge such other duties as pertain to his office, and as shall be prescribed by the Board of Directors.

ARTICLE VIII.
THE CLERK OF CORPORATION.

It shall be the duty of the Clerk to keep a record of all the meetings of the stockholders and of the Board of Directors, if so requested by them; to notify the stockholders of all the stockholders' meetings; to record the votes of the stockholders in a book to be kept for that purpose; and to discharge such other duties as pertain to his office, or may be prescribed by the Board of Directors.

ARTICLE IX.
THE ASSISTANT CLERK OF CORPORATION.

The Assistant Clerk of Corporation shall perform, in the absence of the Clerk, all the duties of that office.

ARTICLE X.
THE BOARD OF DIRECTORS.

At each Annual Meeting of the Stockholders, there shall be chosen from among the stockholders a Board of twenty-six Directors, who shall continue in office for one year, and until others are chosen in their stead.

No person shall be eligible to election as Director who does not own at least one share of stock of this Corporation.

When any Director ceases to be a stockholder, his office shall thereupon become vacant.

The Board of Directors shall elect, by ballot, a President, two Vice-Presidents, and a Treasurer from among their members.

The meetings of the Board shall be held at the call of the President, or of one of the Vice-Presidents, or of three Directors, at such place as may be designated, four days' previous notice having been given in writing to each Director.

Three Directors shall constitute a quorum for the transaction of any business.

It shall be the duty of the Board of Directors to call a meeting of the stockholders at any time, upon the written request of persons representing one-third of the capital stock; and fourteen days' written notice of such meeting shall be given to each stockholder.

The Board of Directors shall determine the form of the Seal of the Corporation, the certificate of stock, and the transfers thereof.

They shall keep a record of all their proceedings, and shall make a report annually to the stockholders, showing the condition of the Corporation.

They shall, either as a board or through committees, audit all accounts, and see that proper books are kept of the business of the Corporation.

They shall audit the accounts of the Treasurer immediately before the Annual Meeting of the Stockholders.

They shall have full charge of the general business and management of the Corporation, shall appoint such committees as they deem advisable and define their duties, and make and authorize all contracts; but all contracts that are in amount one hundred dollars or more shall have to be approved by a majority of the Board.

They shall have the power to accept any resignation and fill all vacancies in their own Board or in the offices of the Corporation, for any unexpired term.

They may appoint and remove at pleasure employees of the Corporation, describe their duties, and fix their compensation.

They shall have the power to lease and purchase any and all lands and buildings necessary or convenient for the transaction of the business of the Corporation, and to make any rules and regulations, not inconsistent with law or with these By-Laws, which they may deem essential to the good of the Corporation.

They shall have, in general, all powers not otherwise vested by law, or by these By-Laws, in the stockholders.

ARTICLE XI.

AMENDMENTS.

These By-Laws may be amended or altered at any meeting of the stockholders, provided that notice of any intended amendments or alterations shall have been given at a previous meeting, or provided that fourteen days' written notice has been given to each stockholder that such intended amendment or alteration is to be acted upon at the Stockholders' Meeting.

CLUB RULES AND REGULATIONS.

MEMBERSHIP.

SECTION 1. No person shall be eligible for membership unless he is a stockholder in the Corporation.

SECT. 2. Members shall affix their names to the Club Book, in which shall be recorded the rules and regulations of the Club, and a provision that subscribers agree to abide by the same.

COMMITTEE ON ADMISSIONS.

A Committee on Admissions shall be chosen, consisting of not less than six, two each from among the Directors residing in Canada, Massachusetts, and New York. Applications of candidates shall state the name, business, and address of applicants, and be proposed by a member in good standing, and indorsed by two others; they must be sent to the Secretary, to be forwarded to the Committee on Admissions in the district in which the candidate resides, who shall make careful examination as to the qualifications and social standing of the applicant. If approved by them, it shall be laid before the Board of Directors for their approval; and, if accepted by them, they shall instruct the Secretary to mail each member a notice, stating the name and address of the candidate, with name of proposer and date of meeting for election. A nine-tenths vote of the members present at such meeting shall be necessary to elect a candidate a member of the Club.

MEETINGS.

The Annual Meeting and Dinner of the Club shall be held in Boston, on the second Tuesday of January of each year, and the regular meetings of the Club at such times and places as shall be determined upon by the Board of Directors.

DUES.

An assessment for annual dues, but not to exceed ten dollars in any one year, shall be made annually upon every member of the Club, for each share of stock that he holds, payable on or before the first day of March of each year.

ARREARS.

Any member who is in arrears for fines, dues, and assessments, and shall neglect to pay the same for thirty days after having received notice of his indebtedness from the Secretary, may be dropped from the roll and from membership by a vote of the Club; and he shall forfeit all rights and privileges while in arrears.

FINES, PENALTIES, AND EXPULSIONS.

SECT. 1. Any member guilty of ungentlemanly conduct, or violation of any of the rules, may be fined, suspended, or expelled by a two-thirds vote at any meeting of the Club; but no action shall be taken unless the member be present, or shall have been duly notified by the Secretary of the charges made against him.

SECT. 2. Any member violating any of the rules or regulations may be fined or suspended by the Board of Directors.

SECT. 3. Any member having been suspended may be reinstated at any meeting of the Club, or at a special meeting called for that purpose by a two-thirds vote of the members present.

SECT. 4. The President or Secretary, at the request in writing of a suspended member, shall call a special meeting of the Club to act on his case, said call to be made within one week after receiving such request.

SECT. 5. Any member having been expelled for violating any of the game or fishery laws, Provincial or State, may be re-elected at an annual meeting only, by a two-thirds vote of all the members present, his reinstatement to take effect at a time to be designated by the President or Board of Directors.

PROPERTY OF THE CORPORATION.

Any injury or damage to the property of the Corporation, or anything in its charge, shall be paid for by the member causing the same.

FREE PERMITS.

Free permits may be issued in the open season to *bona fide* settlers in the vicinity of the lands and waters leased from the Crown, allowing them to fish and hunt over any of the territory which the Corporation has, or may have, obtained the right to fish or hunt over from the Crown Lands Department in the Province of Quebec. Such free permits shall be obtainable from the Club Fish and Game Overseer, and must be countersigned by him, subject to the rules and regulations of the Club. It shall be discretionary with the Overseer to cancel or disallow such permits to any settlers in case of abuse. It shall be considered an abuse of such free permits if a settler wastes or destroys fish, takes more game than is allowed by the Provincial game laws in any one season, or hunts or fishes for the market.

LICENSES.

SECT. 1. The Corporation may issue licenses to any person or persons to hunt, fish, shoot, or take game, or to be or go upon its property, or any portion thereof, at such prices, and for such times, and under such regulations as may be prescribed by the Board of Directors.

SECT. 2. In case any person be licensed to hunt, fish, shoot, or go upon the property owned or leased by the Corporation, and the said person shall offend against any of the rules or regulations of the Corporation, the said person shall forfeit his license, and leave the grounds of the Corporation at once.

GUESTS.

SECT. 1. Guests may be introduced by members to the privileges of the Corporation, or by invitation through the Board of Directors.

SECT. 2. A committee of three shall be appointed by the Board of Directors, to be called the Committee on Guests, who shall have entire charge of the Club House and preserves, in regard to guests; and they shall make such rules for the government of guests, and the fees to be charged, as they may deem advisable from time to time, subject always to the revision and sanction of the Board of Directors and the other printed rules of the Club.

SECT. 3. Members can introduce guests to the privileges of the Club House alone, at any time when the Club House can accommodate them, without displacing members.

SECT. 4. Any member, wishing to introduce a guest at the Club grounds, must send in his own name with the name of the guest to the Secretary, who shall forward the permit for said guest, and keep a record of guests in a book for the purpose.

SECT. 5. The Directors, through the committee, may limit the number of guests to be admitted annually, in case it may become necessary in their judgment so to do.

SECT. 6. Any member introducing a guest to the grounds is responsible for his guest's observance of the rules of the Corporation, and decorum, while the guest is in the grounds of the Corporation.

SECT. 7. The preceding sections (2, 3, 4, and 5) in relation to guests shall not apply to ladies, or boys under sixteen years of age, belonging to families of members; but they shall, as families of members, be entitled to the privileges of the Corporation, under its rules and regulations; neither shall said sections (2, 3, 4, and 5) apply to lady guests.

SECT. 8. No guest shall be admitted to the grounds of the Corporation, unless he is accompanied by the member introducing him; and, upon the departure of the member from the grounds, the privileges of the guest will cease.

HUNTING.

SECT. 1. Every member shall vigorously observe and enforce the game and fishery laws of the Province of Quebec and State of Maine.

SECT. 2. Any member found guilty of violating any of the game or fishery laws, or any portion thereof, in their respective territories, shall be subject to expulsion from the Club at the first meeting following such violation, besides paying the lawful penalty to the Province or State in which the violation took place.

SECT. 3. No member of the Club shall hunt moose, caribou, or deer on the Club preserves with dogs, and no dogs (except bird dogs) shall be admitted upon the territory.

SECT. 4. Members shall use every means possible, in hunting deer, to single out bucks, and spare the does.

SECT. 5. No member of this Club shall shoot more than one moose or two deer (or caribou) on the Club grounds, upon one or both sides of the international boundary, in any one season; and, where a party are camping together, they shall not shoot more deer than is sufficient to supply them with venison, 'and they shall carefully observe that no deer are shot, and their carcasses, or any portion thereof, wasted or thrown away.

SECT. 6. No member of this Club shall shoot more than twenty-five partridges on the Club grounds in any one week during the season.

FISHING.

SECT. 1. No member shall kill any trout, land-locked salmon, or bass, or other game fish, unless he has good reason to believe that it will be used for food.

SECT. 2. No member of this Club shall kill more than fifty trout or fifteen black bass upon the Club preserves in any one day.

SECT. 3. No member of this Club shall send or carry away from the Club premises more than twenty-five pounds of trout, land-locked salmon, or black bass, upon any one visit.

SECT. 4. Trout of less than six inches in length, land-locked salmon less than twelve inches in length, and black bass less than one pound in weight, caught in waters owned or leased by this Club, shall be carefully returned to the water as soon as caught. If such fish die, it shall be scored against the member taking the same, and he may reclaim it.

SECT. 5. Where members are camped together at any of the lakes or streams, they shall not kill more trout than needed to supply the camp, and they shall see that no fish are wasted or thrown away; at such times, also, when fish are plentiful, members are expected to return to the water, as soon as caught, all fish under one-half pound, until they have sufficient for their immediate use, when they shall stop fishing altogether.

SECT. 6. No member shall fish in any manner except with rod and line, but trolling with a spoon for black bass will be allowed in Spider Lake after July 1.

FIRES.

All members shall take great care, especially during the dry season, that no damage is done by fire.

Fires are to be lighted only when necessary for cooking or warmth, and never for amusement.

All combustible substances — such as dry wood, bark, moss, grass, brush, etc. — must be removed from the immediate vicinity of the fire, so that neighboring property shall not be in danger.

No fire shall be left alone for any considerable length of time out of doors, but shall be extinguished before leaving.

GUIDES.

SECT. 1. All members shall have the privilege of taking guides on the Club grounds, but any fish or game killed by said guides shall be scored against said members.

SECT. 2. Members must choose such guides as are sanctioned or recommended by the Board of Directors.

BOATS.

SECT. 1. Members shall be responsible for all damage done to boats while being used by them in fishing, and shall see that the boats are cleaned and properly housed as soon as brought to land.

SECT. 2. If on any day the number of members desiring to fish shall exceed the number of boats belonging to the Club, then the boats shall be apportioned to such members, not to exceed three persons to each boat; but, if the number of members exceed three to each boat, then the privilege to fish shall be decided by lot, unless such members otherwise agree.

REGISTRATION.

Each member shall register upon arrival, and also register in his own hand-writing each day, the number and kind of fish or game killed by him, and the place where killed, said registry to be made the same day. While members are in the camps, they shall keep a daily record, to be entered in the Club register upon their return.

GENERAL RULES.

SECT. 1. All members intending visiting the Club grounds for fishing or hunting should, as far as possible, notify the Fish and Game Overseer and Secretary at least one week previous to their intended visit, and state the time they will arrive, the number expected to form the party, and the number of guides they will require. They should also state what camps they intend to visit, so that everything can be put in readiness for them.

SECT. 2. The Club steamer shall take preference always in meeting members and conveying their baggage to and from the carry, connecting with the steamer on Lake Megantic.

SECT. 3. No member shall, while in camp, make waste of any of the premises leased to the Club; they shall not cut or strip the bark from any trees suitable for saw-logs, but they will be allowed to cut wood for fuel. They shall not interfere with any logs, booms, boats, tools, or any other property belonging to the parties from whom the premises are leased; nor shall they allow any such interference by their guides or friends.

SECT. 4. In order to maintain shelter about the camps, no member nor guide shall cut any wood for fuel standing within ten rods of the camp, nor destroy any trees within said limit.

SECT. 5. No member, in passing along the trails, shall shoot at any mark in the line of said trail.

SECT. 6. Members when taking their departure from the camps must leave everything as found; they shall see that there is cut and piled inside the camp sufficient kindling wood and fuel to last over one night.

COMMITTEES.

SECT. 1. The Board of Directors shall organize the following sub-committees: —
1. Committee on Rooms and Amusements, three.
2. Committee on Guests, three.

3. Committee on Camps, three.
4. Committee on Trails and Roads, three.
5. Committee on Boats, three.
6. Committee on Admissions, six.

SECT. 2. The Committee on Rooms and Amusements shall have charge of the rooms of the Club House, and shall see that they are, at all times during the season for fishing and hunting, in proper and fit condition for the reception and comfort of the Club and its members; and make and keep posted on the bulletin-boards rules for the government of the Club House. They shall make an inventory, annually, of all the property and effects of the Club under their charge, and hand it to the Board of Directors before the annual meeting.

SECT. 3. The Committee on Guests shall, under the sanction of the Board of Directors, frame such rules in relation to guests as shall be deemed advisable from time to time. They shall have such rules printed, and a copy mailed to each member as soon as sanctioned by the Board.

SECT. 4. The Committee on Camps shall have charge of the various camps, and see that they are always kept in good order and repair; and shall make and keep posted in the camps rules for the government of members while in camp, and see that the rules respecting camps are enforced. They shall also make, annually, an inventory of all the effects — such as cooking utensils, dishes, blankets, etc.— in the camp, and hand to the Board of Directors before the annual meeting.

SECT. 5. The Committee on Trails and Roads shall see that the trails are always open and passable, and kept in as good order as the appropriations for that purpose will admit. They shall also report upon the condition of the trails, annually, to the Board of Directors before the annual meeting.

SECT. 6. The Committee on Boats shall have charge of the Club steamer, boat-houses, and all boats, canoes, and appurtenances belonging to the Club. They shall see that the boats, etc., are kept dry and in good order and properly housed, and the rules respecting boats strictly enforced. They shall use all diligence and impartiality in the distribution of boats to members, when the latter outnumber the former, and frame such rules and regulations for their use as they may deem fit. It shall also be their duty to see that proper connections are made between the Club steamer, the steamer on Lake Megantic, and the trains, so that members will not be delayed in going to and from the Club House. They shall also hand an inventory of all the boats in their charge, annually, to the Executive Board before the annual meeting.

SECT. 7. The Committee on Admissions shall consider all communications in reference to persons desiring to join the Club, and make careful examination as to the qualifications and social standing of such applicant. If a majority of the committee is opposed to the admission of the candidate, the name shall not be acted upon; if a majority is in favor, the name shall be reported to the Secretary, to be acted upon in regular form.

LIST OF OFFICERS AND MEMBERS.
BOARD OF DIRECTORS.

Col. GUSTAVUS LUCKE .... Sherbrooke, P.Q.
Hon. HENRY AYLMER .... Richmond, "
RUFUS H. POPE .... Cookshire, "
F. L. WANKLYN .... Montreal, "
A. A. BOYER, M.P.P. .... " "
FRANCIS P. BUCK .... Sherbrooke, "
Major W. A. MOREHOUSE .... " "
G. H. GORDON .... " "
ALEXANDER ROSS .... Gould, "
UBERT K. PETTINGILL .... Boston, Mass.
HEBER BISHOP, M.D. .... " "
Dr. GEORGE C. AINSWORTH .... " "
CHARLES S. HANKS .... Cambridge, "
JAMES N. FRYE .... Boston, "
J. P. BATES .... " "
Col. S. HARRINGTON .... " "
WM. BLODGETT .... " "
FREDERIC A. FOSTER .... " "
Major CHAS. W. HINMAN .... Roslindale, "
ERASTUS WILLARD .... Dorchester, "
I. O. WOODRUFF .... New York, N.Y.
HENRY W. NASON .... Montclair, N.J.
JOHN W. MASON .... New York, N.Y.
F. H. SOUTHWICK .... " "
Hon. ORVILLE D. BAKER .... Augusta, Me.
CHAS. P. HAZELTINE .... Belfast, "

148

OFFICERS.

President, Col. GUSTAVUS LUCKE		Sherbrooke, P.Q.
Vice-Presidents, { UBERT K. PETTINGILL		10 State St., Boston.
{ I. O. WOODRUFF		88 Maiden Lane, New York.
Secretary, HEBER BISHOP, M.D.		Hotel Hoffman, Boston.
Treasurer, WM. BLODGETT		20 Congress St., Boston.
Asst. Clerk of Corporation, HARRY BUTLER		Portland, Me.
Attorney for Canada, Hon. HENRY AYLMER		Richmond, P.Q.
Attorney for United States, CHAS. S. HANKS		209 Washington St., Boston.

MEMBERS.

The following gentlemen have been elected members of the Club: —

NAMES.	BUSINESS.	ADDRESS.
Ainsworth, Dr. Geo. C.	Dentist,	Hotel Hoffman, Boston.
Ainsworth, F. P.	Merchant,	North Amherst, Mass.
Allen, Charles A.	City Engineer,	Worcester, Mass.
Andrews, F. C.	Insurance,	16 Court St., Brooklyn, N.Y.
Andrews, Dr. R. R.	Dentist,	Cambridge, Mass.
Appleton, Wm., M.D.	Physician,	76 Beacon St., Boston.
Aylmer, Hon. Henry	Attorney,	Richmond, P.Q.
Bailey, Cyrus A.	County Treasurer,	Cookshire, P.Q.
Baker, Hon. Orville D.	Attorney-General, Maine,	Augusta, Me.
Ball, Dr. J. W.	Dentist,	241 Columbus Ave., Boston.
Bates, J. P.	Grocer,	680 Washington St., Boston.

NAMES.	BUSINESS.	ADDRESS.
Baxter, Thos.	Builder and Contractor,	Stoneham, Mass.
Bean, Capt. E. D.	With John P. Lovell Arms Co.,	Boston.
Bean, James		Medford, Mass.
Bell, Charles J.	Actor,	34 West 26th St., New York.
Bishop, Heber, M.D.	Physician,	Hotel Hoffman, Boston.
Blodgett, S. C., Jr.	Banker and Broker,	Providence, R.I.
Blodgett, William	Banker and Broker,	20 Congress St., Boston.
Bowles, Edward M.	Manufacturer,	18 Waterford St., Boston.
Boyer, A. A.	Member Legislative Assembly, Quebec,	Montreal, P.Q.
Brown, Edward J.	Cotton Dealer,	9 Oliver St., Boston.
Brown, Frederic L.	Cotton Dealer,	9 Oliver St., Boston.
Briggs, Walter D.	Attorney,	Cambridge, Mass.
Buck, Francis P.	Manufacturer,	Sherbrooke, P.Q.
Burlen, Wm. H.	Leather,	220 Congress St., Boston.
Carolin, Wm. V.	Banker and Broker,	55 Broadway, New York.
Champlin, Albert R.	Lumber Dealer,	Westerly, R.I.
Clapp, Dr. Wright	Dentist,	62 Trinity Terrace, Boston.
Clark, Dwight		Indian Orchard, Mass.
Clousten, C. G.		Metropolitan Club, Montreal, P.Q.
Cochrane, Robert	Attorney,	6 York Chambers, Toronto, Ont.
Congden, Johns H.	Hardware,	Providence, R.I.
Cook, Isaac L., Jr.		Boston.
Cooke, Dr. Fred. A.	Dentist,	Hotel Hoffman, Boston.
Corey, Charles B.	Ornithologist,	8 Arlington St., Boston.
Coté, J. L.	Sherbrooke House,	Sherbrooke, P.Q.
Cowee, C. A.	Heywood Chair Co.,	Gardner, Mass.
Cummings, Thos. H.	Boston *Pilot*,	597 Washington St., Boston.

NAMES.	BUSINESS.	ADDRESS.
Dame, Warren S.	Hardware, Fishing Tackle, etc.,	374 Washington St., Boston.
Dickson, Fred S.	Attorney,	3937 Chestnut St., Philadelphia, Pa.
Donnell, J. C.	Salesman,	383 Washington St., Boston.
Dorr, Frank W.	Attorney,	Newton, Mass.
Douglas, Henry H.		Melrose, Mass.
Eaton, Francis S.		62 Commonwealth Ave., Boston.
Edwards, Chas. R.	Grocer,	Hotel Berkeley, Boston.
Edwards, D. W.	Agent,	418 Washington St., Boston.
Ellis, Augustus H.	Agent,	211 Beacon St., Boston.
Ellsworth. Geo. F.	Hardware,	South Gardner, Mass.
Everett, W. B.	Bicycles, etc.,	8 Berkeley St., Boston.
Fall, Chas. G.	Attorney,	Malden, Mass.
Fenno, Edward N.	Wool,	111 Federal St., Boston.
Ferguson, J. H.	Attorney,	Toronto, Ont.
Fleury, J. S.		New Haven, Conn.
Flint, Albert J.	Attorney,	15 Toronto St., Toronto, Ont.
Foster, Frederic A.	"Eureka" Silk Manufacturer,	104 Arch St., Boston.
Francis, Geo. E., M.D.	Physician,	79 Elm St., Worcester, Mass.
Frye, Jas. N.	Hardware,	16 St. James Ave., Boston.
Gilmore, R. S.	Grocer,	West Broadway, Boston.
Gordon, G. Henry	Railway Contractor,	Sherbrooke, P.Q.
Gould, A. C.	Publisher *Rifle*,	4 Exchange Place, Boston.
Greene, Lyman R.		99 Henry St., Brooklyn, N.Y.
Greene, S. M.		99 Henry St., Brooklyn, N.Y.
Greenwood, Alvin M.	Merchant,	Gardner, Mass.

NAMES.	BUSINESS.	ADDRESS.
Hall, G. F.	Treasurer Nonantum Worsted Co.,	5 Chauncy St., Boston.
Hall, W. L., M.D.	Physician,	32 Salem St., Medford, Mass.
Hall, Wm. P.	Retired,	Belfast, Me.
Hanks, Chas. S.	Attorney,	209 Washington St., Boston.
Harriman, Geo. B.	Dentist,	4 Park St., Boston.
Harrington, Col. S.	Master " Elliot " School,	27 Bowdoin St., Boston.
Hazeltine, Chas. P.	Real Estate,	Belfast, Me.
Henry, George	Watchmaker,	Lennoxville, P.Q.
Heywood. George	Heywood Chair Co.,	Gardner, Mass.
Hills, Wm. S.	Wholesale Flour,	243 South St., Boston.
Hinman, Major Chas. W.	State Inspector Gas and Meters,	32 Hawley St., Boston.
Hovey, Major Chas. L.	Merchant Tailor,	13 Avon St., Boston.
Howe, Dr. Benj. Varnum	Dentist,	106 Tremont St., Boston.
Howe, Geo. E.	Attorney,	23 Court St., Boston.
Hunt, D. F.	Merchant,	Reading, Mass.
Hunt, H. N.	Merchant,	8 India St., Boston.
Hutchinson, Winfred S.	Attorney,	53 Devonshire St., Boston.
Ingraham, George	Insurance,	3 East 12th St., New York.
Kendall, Ralph M.	Hardware, Cutlery, Fishing Tackle, etc.,	374 Washington St., Boston.
Kilham, Chas. A.	Wholesale Druggist,	356 Washington St., Boston.
Knowlton, Chas. L.	Retired,	Belfast, Me.
Langdon, H. S.	Leather,	Newton, Mass.
Langley, E. M.	Salesman,	304 River St., Cambridgeport, Mass.
Lawrence, Robt. B.	Attorney,	Mills Building, Wall St., New York.
Leckie, R. G.	Agent,	Sherbrooke, P.Q.
Lucke, Col. Gustavus	Hardware,	Sherbrooke, P.Q.

NAMES.	BUSINESS.	ADDRESS.
Manning, H. S.	Railway Supplies,	111 Liberty St., New York.
Mason, John W.	Wool,	142 Duane St., New York.
Mason, Wm. P.	Wool,	142 Duane St., New York.
Maxon, C. Clarence	Lumber Dealer,	Westerly, R.I.
McElrath, Percy	Attorney,	45 William St., New York.
McFee, D. E.	Supt. International Railway,	Sherbrooke, P.Q.
Means, James	Leather,	133 St. Botolph St., Boston.
Miller, J. Ferdinand	Book-keeper,	70 Station St., Roxbury, Mass.
Morehouse, Major W. A.	Publisher *Examiner*,	Sherbrooke, P.Q.
Morgan, Geo. Middleton	With Henry W. Peabody & Co..	Boston.
Morris, M. A., M.D.	Physician,	308 Main St., Charlestown, Mass.
Nash, N. C.	Revere Sugar Refining Co.,	19 Cragie St., Cambridge, Mass.
Nason, Henry W.	Banker and Broker,	74 Broadway, New York.
Noyes, David W.	Gents' Furnishing Goods,	Washington St., Boston.
Partridge, E. E.	Insurance,	70 State St., Boston.
Paterson, R. McD.	Insurance,	Phœnix Assurance Co., Montreal, P.Q.
Perkins, Seth	Superintendent City Hall,	Boston.
Pettingill, Ubert K.	Advertising.	10 State St., Boston.
Pillsbury, Hon. Edwin L.	Senator,	305 Main St., Charlestown, Mass.
Pope, Rufus H.		Cookshire, P.Q.
Price, Linus M.	Banker,	Com'l Nat'l Bank, Broadway, New York.
Quincy, C. F.		17 Temple Pl., Boston.
Rabbeth, F. J.	Inventor.	Hotel Warren, Roxbury, Mass.
Raymond, Walter	Raymond's Vacation Excursions,	296 Washington St., Boston.
Richardson, Wm. M.	Attorney,	Equitable Building, Boston.

NAMES.	BUSINESS.	ADDRESS.
Robinson, Arthur W.	Publisher,	83 Winter St., Boston.
Robinson, Henry W.	Attorney,	50 State St., Boston.
Rogers, Winthrop L.	With Henry W. Peabody & Co.,	819 Marlboro St., Boston.
Ross, Alexander	Merchant,	Gould, P.Q.
Rowell, Chas. A.	Merchant Tailor,	302 Washington St., Boston.
Russell, Robert S.	Wool,	200 Devonshire St., Boston.
Rust, E. Hyde	Asbestos,	169 Congress St., Boston.
Sanborn, Henry W.		Brighton, Mass.
Schoff, A. H.	Merchant,	41 Worth St., New York.
Schoff, Alfred	Greenfield House,	Greenfield, Mass.
Shaw, E. A.	Cotton Buyer,	48 Congress St., Boston.
Shaw, H. M.		Rockland, Mass.
Slade, D. D., M.D.	Physician,	Chestnut Hill, Mass.
Small, L. T.	Instructor Y. M. C. A. Gymnasium,	Hotel Hoffman, Boston.
Smith, J. F.	Queen's Counsel,	Toronto, Ont.
Smith, Nat'l S.	Attorney,	95 Nassau St., New York.
Southwick, F. H.	Merchant,	29 White St., New York.
Spencer, Edward L.	Attorney,	Warren St., cor. Church, New York.
Spooner, D. W.	Manufacturer,	435 Columbus Ave., Boston.
Stevens, Dr. S. G.	Dentist,	175 Tremont St., Boston.
Stevens, Wm. B.	District Attorney, Middlesex,	200 Washington St., Boston.
Stevens, W. F., M.D.	Physician,	Stoneham, Mass.
Stimpson, Henry Quincy		63 Chatham St., Boston.
Stoddard, O. H. S.,	Cutlery, Hardware, Fishing Tackle, etc.,	374 Washington St., Boston.
Strather, George K.		Gardner, Mass.
Stratton, Herbert S.	Merchant,	Gardner, Mass.
Sweet, Henry N.	With Henry W. Peabody & Co.,	70 Kilby St., Boston.

NAMES.	BUSINESS.	ADDRESS.
Taylor, Alexander, Jr.	Banker and Broker.	Mamaroneck, N.Y.
Taylor, Chas. F., M.D.	Publisher *Medical World*,	1590 Chestnut St., Philadelphia, Pa.
Thomas, Daniel	City Registrar,	Sherbrooke, P.Q.
Thorne, T.	Attorney,	Toronto, Ont.
Tilney, Robt. F.	Merchant,	59 Liberty St., New York.
Tufts, Nathan F.	Merchant,	Charlestown, Mass.
Turner, Augustus W., M.D.	Physician,	12 Upton St., Boston.
Wadsworth, Wm. B.	Broker,	44 New St., New York.
Wanklyn, F. L.	Asst. Supt. Locomotive Dept. G. T. Ry.,	St. James Club, Montreal, P.Q.
Wells, Jas. S. C.	Mining Engineer,	Columbia College, 49th St., New York.
Wemyss, Jas., Jr.	Furniture,	82 Canal St., Boston.
Weston, Edward	Express Agent.	298 Border St., East Boston.
Wheelock, Chas. G.	Manufacturing, Printing, &c.,	48 Oliver St., Boston.
Wilbur, Harry N.	Chocolate Manufacturer,	Philadelphia, Pa.
Wilbur, H. O.	Chocolate Manufacturer,	Philadelphia, Pa.
Willard, Erastus	Celluloid,	40 Summer St., Boston.
Woodruff, Galen	Druggist,	500 Tremont St., Boston.
Woodruff, I. O.	Physicians' Specialties,	88 Maiden Lane, New York.
Woodruff, Jas. E.	Chemicals,	48 & 50 Lake St., Chicago, Ill.
Woodruff, T. T.	Attorney,	Sears Building, Boston.
Woodward, J. R.	General Manager Q. C. Railway,	Sherbrooke, P.Q.
Yenetchie, Geo. V.	Grocer,	142 Blackstone St., Boston.

QUEBEC GAME LAWS.

MOOSE, CARIBOU, DEER.

1. It is forbidden, within this Province, to hunt, kill or take:
(1) Moose and deer, between the first day of February and the first day of September in each year. [Amended May, 1887, so as to read, "between the first day of January and the first day of October in each year," making the CLOSE SEASON two months longer.]
(2) The female of the moose, at any time until the fifteenth day of October, one thousand eight hundred and eighty-eight, after which date the close season shall be the same as for the male moose. [Amended May, 1887, so as to read, "moose (male or female), *at any time* UNTIL OCTOBER 1, 1890."]
(3) Caribou, between the first day of March and the first day of September in each year. [Amended May, 1887, so as to read, "between the first day of January and first day of October of each year," making the close time the same as for deer.]
2. After the first ten days of the close season, all railways, steamboat and other companies, and public carriers, are forbidden, during the remainder of such close season, to carry the whole or any part of any moose, caribou, or deer; and any railway, steamboat, or other company, or any person favoring in any manner whatever the contravention of this section, shall be liable to a penalty. [Amended May, 1887, so as to read, "After the first ten days of the close season, all railways and steamboat companies and public carriers are forbidden to carry the whole or any part (except the skin) of any moose, caribou, or deer, without being authorized thereto by the Commissioner of Crown Lands."]
3. No person shall have a right, unless domiciled in this Province, and he has previously obtained a permit from the Commissioner of Crown Lands for that purpose, to kill or take alive, during one season's hunting, more than two moose, three deer, or two caribou.

This prohibition, however, applies to Indians, only when it does not seriously affect their means of subsistence. [Amended May, 1887, so as to read, "No person (whitemen or Indians) has a right, during one season's hunting, to kill or take alive — unless he has previously obtained a permit from the Commissioner of Crown Lands for that purpose — more than three caribou and four deer.

"N. B.— The hunting of moose, caribou or deer with dogs, or by means of snares, traps, etc., is prohibited."]

BEAVER, MINK, OTTER, MARTEN, PEKAN, HARE, MUSKRAT.

4. It is forbidden to hunt, kill or take:
(1) Any beaver, mink, otter, marten or pekan between the first day of April and the first day of November in each year.
(2) Any hare, between the first day of February and the first day of November in each year.
(3) Any muskrat, between the first day of May in each year and the first day of April following, but only in the counties of Maskinongé, Yamaska, Richelieu and Berthier.

WOODCOCK, PARTRIDGE, SNIPE, BLACK DUCK, WILD DUCK, TEAL, ETC.

5. It is also forbidden—
(1) To hunt, kill or take:
   a. Any woodcock, snipe, or partridge of any kind, between the first day of February and the first day of September in each year.
   b. Any black duck, teal, or wild duck of any kind, except sheldrake and gull, between the fifteenth day of April and the first day of September in each year.
   c. Any of the birds above mentioned, except partridge, at any time between one hour after sunset and one hour before sunrise; and during such prohibited hours it is also forbidden to keep exposed, under any pretext, lures or decoys near a cache, boat or bank.

(2) To disturb, injure, gather or take, at any time, the eggs of any species of wild fowl, the hunting of which is prohibited by this section, as well as those of the wild swan, wild goose or Canada goose: and all vessels or boats employed in disturbing, gathering or taking the eggs of any species of the aforesaid wild fowl, may, as well as the eggs, be confiscated and sold.

Nevertheless, in that part of the Province to the east and north of the counties of Bellechasse and Montmorency, the inhabitants may at any time, but only for the purpose of procuring food, hunt, kill or take any of the birds mentioned in paragraph b of this section.

6. It is forbidden to take, at any time, by means of ropes, snares, springs, cages, nets, pits or traps of any kind, any of the animals or birds, the hunting of which is prohibited by Sections 1 and 5, except partridges, and to place, construct, erect or set, either wholly or in part, any engine for such purpose; and any person finding any

engine so placed, constructed, erected or set, of whatever nature it may be, may take possession of or destroy the same, as well as any snare or trap set or extended to take the fur bearing animals mentioned in Section 4 of this act, when such snares or traps remain so set or extended during the time when the hunting of such animals is prohibited.

It is also forbidden, in hunting any of the birds mentioned in Section 5, to make use of any fire-arm of a less calibre than 8.

INSECTIVOROUS AND OTHER BIRDS BENEFICIAL TO AGRICULTURE, ETC.

7. It is forbidden, between the first day of March and the first day of September, in any year, to shoot, kill or take, by means of nets, traps, springs, snares, cages or otherwise, any of the birds known as perchers, such as swallows, king-birds, warblers, flycatchers, woodpeckers, whip-poor-wills, finches (song-sparrows, red-birds, indigo birds, etc.), cow-buntings, titmice, goldfinches, grives (robins, wood-thrushes, etc.), kinglets, bobolinks, bobolinks, grakles, grosbeaks, humming birds, cuckoos, owls, etc., or to take their nests or eggs, except eagles, falcons, hawks and other birds of the *falconidae*, wild pigeons, kingfishers, crows, ravens, waxwings (*recollets*), shrikes, jays, magpies, sparrows and starlings; and whosoever finds any nets, traps, springs, snares, cages, etc., so placed or set, may take possession of or destroy the same.

This section does not, however, apply to poultry.

8. It is forbidden to hunt migratory quail until the thirty-first of December, one thousand eight hundred and eighty-six.

GENERAL PROVISIONS.

9. It is forbidden, at all times, to use or employ strychnine or other deleterious poison, either mineral or vegetable, or any spring-gun, to hunt or take, kill or destroy any animal mentioned in this act.

10. Every game-keeper shall forthwith seize all animals or birds mentioned in the preceding sections, or any portions of such animals or birds,—except the skin when the animal has been killed during the time when hunting is allowed,—found by him in the possession or custody or in the care of any person during any close season, or which appear to him to have been taken or killed during such period, or by any of the illegal means set forth in Sections 6 and 9 of this act, and bring them before any justice of the peace, who shall, if proved that the law has been broken, declare them confiscated, either in whole or in part, for the benefit of the Province.

But every such animal, or any portion thereof, may be bought or sold, when lawfully taken, during ten days, to be computed from the expiration of the various periods respectively fixed by this act for the taking or killing thereof.

However, the birds, the hunting of which is prohibited by the first part of Section 7, and the animals enumerated in the preceding sections, are exempt from such seizure and confiscation, when kept alive; but, in the latter case, the proof that no contravention of the law has taken place shall be upon and at the charges of the proprietor or possessor of such animals.

11. Every game-keeper may cause to be opened or may himself open, in case of refusal, any bag, parcel, chest, box, trunk, or other receptacle (outside the limits mentioned in the following section), in which he has reason to believe that game, killed or taken during the close season, or peltries out of season, are kept.

12. Every game-keeper, if he have reason to suspect, and if he suspect, that game, killed or taken during the close season, or peltries out of season, are contained or kept in any private house, store, shed, or other buildings, shall make a deposition before a justice of the peace, and demand a search-warrant to search such store, private house, shed, or other building, and thereupon such justice of the peace is bound to issue a warrant.

13. Every game-keeper shall, after each seizure and confiscation, cause to be established, as soon as possible, by a competent person, duly sworn, the condition of the article or articles so seized and confiscated, place them in a safe place, and then immediately report to the Department of Crown Lands.

The proprietor of such articles so seized and confiscated, or his attorney or mandatary *ad hoc*, may, within the delays prescribed by Section 15 of this act, himself also appoint, at his own expense, a person who shall have a right to examine such articles.

But if the proprietor or his attorney or mandatary *ad hoc* be not present, and cannot be found at the time of such seizure and confiscation, notice thereof shall be given twice, during fifteen days, in a newspaper published in the French language, and twice in a newspaper published in the English language, in the place where such seizure and confiscation took place, or in the nearest place, if no such newspapers are published in such place; and the costs of such notice shall be at the expense of the proprietor or of his attorney or his mandatary *ad hoc*, if the articles be claimed; if not, they shall be paid by the game-keeper to whom, at the expiration of the said delay, the said article or articles, so seized and confiscated, shall belong.

PENALTIES, PROCEEDINGS, ETC.

14. Every infringement of any of the provisions of this act is punishable summarily upon prosecution, which may be brought either by the game-keeper or by any other person before a justice of the peace of the district in which the offense was committed, or the seizure and confiscation effected; and the provisions of the act of the Parliament

of Canada. 32-33 Victoria. Chapter 31, respecting the duties of justices of the peace, out of sessions, in relation to summary convictions, and the provisions of Chapter 103 of the Consolidated Statutes of Canada, shall, unless incompatible, apply to all prosecutions brought under this act.

The fines are :—

For every infringement, $2 to $100, or imprisonment in default of payment.

Such justice of the peace shall, if he find the proof sufficient, impose the fine with costs, which fine wholly belongs to the prosecutor if he be a game-keeper, and one-half only if he do not act in an official capacity; in the latter case, the other half is paid over to the game-keeper for the division to belong to him.

In default of immediate payment, the offender is imprisoned in the common gaol of the district within the limits of which the offense was committed, or in which the seizure and confiscation were effected, for any period of time not exceeding three months, and, in case of infringement of Section 9, for a period not exceeding six months.

Every justice of the peace has power to convict on view.

Seizures, confiscations and prosecutions are at the risk of the person who caused the same to be made or carried on.

15. No proceeding under this act shall be quashed, annulled or set aside by *certiorari*; but an appeal may, within ten days, be brought before the Circuit Court of the district in which the offense took place, or the seizure and confiscation were effected, in the same manner as appeals under the Municipal Code, if the proprietor or his attorney or mandatary *ad hoc* be present at the time of such seizure and confiscation, when the proceedings are for such seizure and confiscation; but, when the proprietor or his attorney or mandatary is not present, the right of appeal remains during the whole of the delay required by the notice mentioned in Section 13 of this act.

A similar delay of ten days to appeal exists respecting the fine.

The government of the Province cannot be held to be responsible for any costs incurred in virtue of such proceedings.

16. Nor prosecution shall be brought after three calendar months from the day of the committing of the offense charged.

APPOINTMENTS, GAME LICENSES, ETC.

17. There shall be, for the purpose of specially insuring the execution of this act and of all other acts respecting hunting which may be passed in future for this Province, a game superintendent appointed by the Commissioner of Crown Lands.

Such officer shall be chosen from among the permanent employees of the Department of Crown Lands.

18. The Commissioner of Crown Lands has also the power of appointing persons to see to the observance of this act, and of any act which may hereafter be passed relating to game in this Province, and to assign to them any territory or division which he may, under the circumstances, deem advisable.

These persons are to be called game-keepers; and the Commissioner of Crown Lands may, in certain cases, restrict as far as they are concerned, and also as far as other game-keepers under his control are concerned, the powers conferred upon them by this act.

19. No person, who is not domiciled in the Province of Quebec nor in that of Ontario, can, at any time, hunt in this Province, within the meaning of this act, without being authorized thereto by license to that effect.

20. Such permit may, on payment of a fee of twenty dollars, be granted by the Commissioner of Crown Lands to any person, not domiciled in either of the said Provinces, who shall apply to him therefor, and is valid for a whole shooting season; it shall be countersigned by the game superintendent. It shall be lawful, however, for the Lieutenant-Governor in Council, in exceptional cases, to grant hunting permits gratuitously, or for a fee less than twenty dollars. [Amended May, 1887, making the fee $10 for members of a Fish and Game Club incorporated in the Province of Quebec under the provisions of Act 48 Vict., Chap. 12. Permits are not transferable.]

21. The Commissioner of Crown Lands may grant written permits to any person or persons who may be *bona fide* desirous of obtaining birds, eggs or fur bearing animals for scientific purposes, to procure them for that purpose during the close season, and such permits shall be countersigned by the game superintendent; and the person who shall have obtained such permit shall not be liable to any penalty under this act, provided he send in to the Department of Crown Lands, at the expiration of such permit, a solemn declaration showing the species and number of the birds, eggs or fur bearing animals so procured by him for scientific purposes.

22. All Crown land agents or Crown timber agents and all wood-rangers, appointed by the Commissioner of Crown Lands, are, while in office as such, *ex-officio* game-keepers for the divisions under their respective superintendence, and are not entitled to any additional salary for such service.

23. Every game-keeper shall, at the end of each of the months of March, June, September and December, in each year, forward to the Department of Crown Lands a report of his proceedings during the previous quarter, and of the infringements of the law which have come to his knowledge during the same period.

24. The Lieutenant-Governor in Council may, in his discretion, prohibit the hunting or killing of any bird or fur bearing animal, for a period not exceeding five years.

25. All former acts and parts of acts, relating to game in this Province, are hereby repealed.

26. The present act shall be known as "The Quebec Game Law," and shall come into force on the day of its sanction.

EXTRACTS FROM THE
DOMINION OF CANADA FISHERY LAWS AND REGULATIONS.

The following extracts from the Dominion Fishery Laws and Regulations are selected principally for the information of lessees of rivers and lakes in the Province of Quebec, and anglers generally.

For complete copies of these laws and regulations, application should be made to the Fisheries Department, Ottawa.

31 VICT., CHAP. 60.

SECT. 7. It shall be lawful to fish for, catch and kill salmon with a rod and line, in the manner known as fly surface fishing, between the thirtieth day of April and the thirty-first day of August, in the Province of Quebec.

Sub-sect. 3. Foul or unclean salmon shall not be at any time caught or killed.

Sub-sect. 4. Salmon fry, parr and smolt, shall not be at any time fished for, caught or killed, and no salmon or grilse of less weight than three pounds shall be caught or killed; but, where caught by accident in nets lawfully used for other fish, they shall be liberated alive at the cost and risk of the owner of the fishery, on whom shall, in every case, devolve the proof of such actual liberation.

Sub-sect. 6. The use of nets or other apparatus which capture salmon shall, except in the Provinces of Nova Scotia and New Brunswick, be confined to tidal waters.

Sub-sect. 7. The Minister, or any Fishery Officer authorized to such effect, shall have power to define the tidal boundary of estuary fishing for the purposes of this act; and, above the actual limit so to be laid down, it shall be unlawful, without the special fishery lease or license above provided for, to fish for salmon, except with a rod and line, in the manner known as fly surface fishing, under a penalty not to exceed one hundred dollars, and imprisonment, in default of payment, for any term not exceeding two months.

Sub-sect. 11. Except in the manner known as fly surface fishing with a rod and line, salmon shall not be fished for, caught or killed by any artificial pass or salmon leap, nor in any pool where salmon spawn.

Sub-sect. 12. Except under the authority and for the special purpose provided for in this act, no one shall take, buy, sell, destroy, use or possess any salmon roe, nor injure any spawning bed.

LAKE AND RIVER TROUT FISHERY.

SECT. 8. It shall not be lawful to fish for, catch or kill any kind of trout (or "lunge") in any way whatever between the first day of October and the first day of January; and no one shall, at any time, fish for, catch or kill trout by other means than angling by hand with hook and line, in any inland lake, river, or stream, except in tidal waters.

WHITEFISH AND SALMON TROUT FISHERY.

SECT. 9. It shall not be lawful to fish for or catch whitefish in any manner between the nineteenth day of November and the first day of December, nor by means of any kind of seine, between the thirty-first day of July and the first day of December, in the Province of Quebec, nor shall the fry of the same be at any time destroyed.

Sub-sect. 2. Gill nets for catching salmon trout or whitefish shall have meshes of at least five inches extension measure; and gill nets shall not be set within two miles of any seining ground.

Sub-sect. 3. Seines for catching whitefish shall have meshes of not less than four inches extension measure.

BASS AND PICKEREL FISHERY.

SECT. 10. Close seasons for bass, pike, pickerel (*doree*), maskinonge, and other fish, may be fixed by the Governor in Council, to suit different localities.

POSSESSION OF FISH.

SECT. 11. No one shall, without lawful excuse, the proof of which shall devolve wholly on the party charged, buy, sell or possess any fish named in this act, or parts thereof, caught or killed during seasons when and by means whereof catching or killing the same is prohibited by law.

Sub-sect. 2. It shall be the duty of every customs officer, excise officer, police officer or constable, clerk of a market or other party in charge of any market place in any village, town or city, to seize and forfeit on view to his own proper use, or gift, any fish enumerated in this act, caught or killed during prohibited seasons, or which appears to have been killed by unlawful means; but every such seizure and appropriation, with the date, place and circumstance thereof, shall be duly reported, together with the name, residence and calling of the person in whose possession such fish was found, to the Fishery Officer having jurisdiction over the district within which such seizure, forfeiture and appropriation have taken place.

SYNOPSIS OF THE FISHERY LAWS

REGARDING CLOSE SEASONS IN THE POVINCE OF QUEBEC.

It is Unlawful to Take

1. Salmon (angling) .... From 1st September to 1st May.
    "   " (Restigouche River) .... " 15th August to 1st May.
2. Speckled trout (*Salmo fontinalis*) .... " 1st October to 1st January.
3. Large grey trout, lunge, and winninish .... " 15th October to 1st December.
4. Pickerel .... " 15th April to 15th May.
5. Bass and maskinonge .... " 15th April to 15th June.
6. Whitefish .... " 10th November to 1st December.

Fine of $5 to $20, or imprisonment in default of payment.

No person may, during their respective close seasons, fish for, catch, kill, buy, sell, or have in possession, any of the kinds of fish mentioned above. Any person doing so is liable to be fined or imprisoned.

N. B.— Angling by hand (with hook and line) is the *only* means permitted to be used for taking fish in the waters of the lakes and rivers under the control of the Government of the Province of Quebec.

Angling must be suspended from six o'clock Saturday night until six o'clock Monday morning.

No person, who is not domiciled in the Province of Quebec, can, at any time, fish in the lakes or rivers of this Province, *not actually under lease*, without having previously obtained a permit to that effect from the Commissioner of Crown Lands. Fee $10. Such permit is valuable for a fishing season, and is not transferable. But no fee shall be required from members of a Club fishing in waters under lease to said Club. . . .

CONSTRUCTION OF FISHWAYS.

SECT. 12. Every dam, slide or other obstruction, across or in any stream where the Minister may determine it to be necessary for the public interest that a fish-pass should exist, shall be provided by the owner or occupier with a durable and efficient fishway, to be maintained in practical and effective condition, in whatever place and of whatever form and capacity will admit of the passage of fish through the same (which place, form and capacity any Fishery Officer may by written notice determine), under a penalty of four dollars for each day during which any such obstruction remains unprovided with a fishway, after three days' notice in writing to the owner or occupier thereof.

Sub-sect. 2. Fishways shall be kept open and unobstructed, and be supplied with a sufficient quantity of water to fulfill the purposes of this enactment, during such times as may be required by any Fishery Officer.

Sub-sect. 3. The Minister may authorize the payment of one-half of the expenses incurred by such owner or occupier in constructing and maintaining any fishway.

Sub-sect. 4. Should it be expedient to procure the construction of any fishway pending proceedings against any owner or occupier for the penalty imposed by this act, the Minister may give directions to make and complete the same forthwith, and to enter upon the premises with the necessary workmen, means and materials, and may recover from the owner or occupier the whole expense so incurred, by action before any competent tribunal.

Sub-sect. 5. No person shall injure or obstruct any fishway, nor do anything to deter or hinder fish from entering and ascending or descending the same, nor injure or obstruct any authorized barrier.

SECT. 14, Sub-sec. 2. Lime, chemical substances or drugs, poisonous matter (liquid or solid), dead or decaying fish, or any other deleterious substance, shall not be drawn into, or allowed to pass into, be left or remain in any water frequented by any of the kinds of fish mentioned in this act; and sawdust or mill-rubbish shall not be drifted or thrown into any stream frequented by fish, under a penalty not exceeding one hundred dollars; provided always that the Minister shall have power to exempt from the operation of this sub-section, wholly or from any portion of the same, any stream or streams in which he considers that its enforcement is not requisite for the public interest.

SYNOPSIS OF QUEBEC FISHERIES ACT.

1. The Commissioner of Crown Lands, or any officer or agent under him authorized to that effect, may grant leases of such of the public lands of the Crown as are situated along the banks of such rivers and lakes in the

Province of Quebec, where the exclusive right of fishing is vested in the Crown as the riparian proprietor, at such rates and subject to such conditions, regulations and restrictions as may from time to time be established by the Lieutenant-Governor in Council, and which shall be published in the *Quebec Official Gazette.*

2. No lease shall be so granted for a period longer than five years from the date thereof; and, in the case of lands situate along rivers known as "salmon rivers," leases therefor shall be made only to and in favor of the highest bidder, after the same shall have been put up at public competition, of which at least one month's notice shall be given in the *Quebec Official Gazette*, and in such other way as to the Commissioner of Crown Lands may seem the most advantageous.

Provided always that the price offered be at least equal to the upset price fixed by the Commissioner, and that, if not sold, the Commissioner may afterwards, by private sale, dispose of the said leases at such upset price, or for a greater sum.

Whenever a lease of lands, previously under lease to one person, is adjudged to another person, the new lessee shall be held to indemnify the previous lessee for the real and not artificial value of any necessary buildings or improvements existing on the land leased, which value, in case of any difference of opinion, shall be definitely fixed and determined by the Commissioner of Crown Lands; and such new lessee shall not be entitled to receive a lease until he shall have furnished proof that he has so indemnified the previous lessee.

And if, in consequence of any incorrectness of survey or other error or cause whatsoever, a lease is found to comprise lands included in a lease of a prior date, the lease last granted shall be void, in so far as it interferes with the one previously issued; and the holder or proprietor of the lease so rendered void shall have no claim for indemnity or compensation by reason of such avoidance.

3. Such license shall confer, for the time being, on the lessee, the right to take and keep the exclusive possession of the lands therein described, subject to such regulations and restrictions as may be established, and shall vest in him the right to fish in the waters thereto adjoining, at such times and in such manner as may be regulated and allowed by any law or statute of the Parliament of Canada then in force, or by any regulations passed in virtue thereof.

It shall also entitle the lessee to institute in his own name any action or suit at law against any wrongful possessor or trespasser, and to prosecute the same, and to recover damages, if any there be.

4. Each lessee shall be bound to establish and maintain, on and over the territory covered by his lease, an efficient guardianship, to secure a complete protection of the fishery rights belonging to it.

He shall further be answerable for damages done to the timber growing on the said territory and in the adjoining territory, by himself or the people under his control, either from waste or from want of sufficient precautions in lighting, watching over or putting out fires; and it shall be incumbent upon him, in case of damage done by fire, to prove that all such precautions have been taken.

5. No lessee shall have the right to sublet any privilege granted him under the provisions of this act, without first notifying the Department of Crown Lands, and receiving the written consent of the Commissioner or of some other person authorized to that effect.

6. The rental shall be paid in advance, and any lessee who fails to do so shall not be entitled to claim the renewal of his lease. The lease of any person convicted of an infraction of this act, or who has violated any regulations under it, may be annulled by the Commissioner of Crown Lands.

7. The Lieutenant-Governor in Council may, if he considers it expedient for the better protection of the Provincial fisheries, divide the Province into fishery divisions, and may appoint a fishery overseer for each such division, whose duties shall be defined by the regulations made under this act.

8. Except in the discharge of any duty imposed by law, no person shall enter upon or pass over the land described in such lease without permission of the lessee or his representative, on pain of incurring a fine of not less than one nor more than ten dollars, and, in default of immediate payment, of an imprisonment not exceeding one month. It shall be lawful, nevertheless, whenever any such land is included in any timber license, that the holder thereof shall have at all times the right to cut and take away all trees, timber and lumber, within the limits of his license and during the term thereof; and it shall further be lawful for him to make use of any floatable river or watercourse, and of any lake, pond or other body of water, and the banks thereof, for the conveyance of all kinds of lumber, and for the passage of all boats, ferries and canoes required therefor,— subject to the charge of repairing all damages resulting from the exercise of such right.

The present section shall not apply to any person simply passing over the said land, or engaged in any occupation not inconsistent with the provisions of this act.

9. If any person, without permission of the lessee or his representative, fishes or employs or induces any other person to fish or assist in fishing in the waters adjoining any such leased land, or removes or carries away or employs or induces or assists any other person to remove or carry away any fish caught in any such waters, he shall not acquire any right to the fish so caught, but the same shall be forfeited and become the absolute property of the lessee, and any such person shall therefor incur a penalty of not less than five nor more than twenty dollars, and, in default of immediate payment, of an imprisonment not exceeding one month.

10. Except for offences to which penalties are already attached, each and every offender against the provisions of this act or regulations made under it shall incur for each offence a penalty of not more than twenty dollars, besides all costs, and, in default of immediate payment, shall be imprisoned for a period not exceeding one month. Contravention on any day of any of the provisions of this act or of any regulations made under it shall constitute a separate offence, and may be punished accordingly.

11. One-half of every penalty imposed by virtue of this act shall belong to Her Majesty for the uses of the Province, and the remaining half shall be paid to the prosecutor, together with the costs which he may have incurred. Each penalty or forfeiture imposed by this act, or by the regulations made thereunder, may be recovered on parol complaint before any Fishery Officer or other magistrate, or before any Crown Lands agent, or other officer or employee of the Crown Lands Department, in a summary manner, on the oath of one credible witness. Any Fishery Officer, or other official mentioned in this section, may convict upon his own view for any of the offences mentioned in this act.

12. The Lieutenant-Governor in Council may, from time to time, vary, amend, and alter all and every regulation as shall be found necessary or deemed expedient for the better management and regulation of such land as is leased under the operation of this act, and the fishing rights thereto pertaining, and such regulations shall have the same force and effect as if herein contained and enacted. Every offence against any such regulation may be stated as having been made in contravention of this act; and, for the purposes of enforcing the same, Fishery Overseers, as well as all agents for the sale of Crown Lands, all employees of the Department of Crown Lands, and all wood rangers, and other persons employed by the Department of Crown Lands, shall be *ex-officio* Justices of the Peace.

13. The remuneration of the Fishery Overseers, and of all other persons employed to perform any duty imposed by this act or by the regulations made under it, shall be determined by the Commissioner of Crown Lands, either by commission or otherwise, and in either case shall be paid out of the proceeds of the operations of this act.

14. It shall be lawful for the Commissioner of Crown Lands, or any officer thereto authorized by him, to grant permits to fish in any waters adjoining lands not under lease, for a period not exceeding one month, upon such terms and subject to such restrictions and conditions as shall be provided by order in Council to that effect.

15. *Bona fide* residents may fish in such unleased rivers as are known not to contain salmon, and in unleased lakes, without first obtaining the permit mentioned in the preceding section.

LEASES OF PUBLIC LANDS.

2. The Commissioner of Crown Lands may, upon the recommendation of the lessees of fishing rights, or without such recommendation, appoint as many guardians as may be deemed necessary for the effectual protection of the fisheries in the different rivers and lakes under his control.

Such guardians shall be sworn to the faithful discharge of their duties, and especially to prevent the taking or killing, or attempting to take or kill, fish in the waters under their charge by illegal means, or at times when the taking or killing of fish is prohibited by law.

They shall be employed for such length of time as the Commissioner of Crown Lands shall consider necessary, and their services shall be paid for by the lessees.

3. It shall be made a condition of leases of lands conveying fishing rights that lessees shall, as soon as possible after the close of each angling season, transmit to the Department of Crown Lands a statement of the number and weight of fish caught in the waters affected by such leases.

4. Leases of lands to convey fishing rights shall be made subject to a general right of passage to and from the water in favor of the occupants, if any, under title from the Crown, of the lands immediately in rear of those leased.

6. Excessive or wasteful fishing or killing of salmon or trout shall involve the cancellation of the lease covering the waters in which it has taken place; and the lessee who has been guilty of such excessive or wasteful fishing shall not be eligible to receive another lease of fishing rights or permit or license to fish within this Province.

7. It shall be lawful for the Lieutenant-Governor in Council, upon the recommendation of the Commissioner of Crown Lands, to reserve from lease for one or more years, for purposes of improvement, any river or lake not leased, or part thereof, the exclusive right of fishing in which is vested in the Crown.

8. The Commissioner of Crown Lands may, with the consent of the owners, and for purposes of management only, assume the control of fishing rights pertaining to granted lands fronting on any river or lake, with a view to improving or leasing the same in connection with those pertaining to ungranted lands fronting on the same river or lake, and paying over to the private owners of such fishing rights a proportionate share of the rent received for the whole.

AN ABSTRACT OF THE

FISH AND GAME LAWS OF THE STATE OF MAINE FOR 1884.

GAME.

(*R. S., Chapter 30.*)

BOUNTY ON WOLVES AND BEARS.

SECT. 5. A bounty of five dollars for every wolf and bear killed in any town shall be paid by the treasurer thereof to the person killing it, upon compliance with the following condition.

SECT. 6. No bounty shall be paid unless the claimant, within ten days after he has killed such animal, or has returned from the hunting in which he killed it, exhibits to the town treasurer the entire skin thereof, with the ears and nose thereon, in as perfect a state as when killed, except natural decay, and signs and makes oath to a certificate, which oath said treasurer may administer, in which he shall state that he killed such animal, and the time and place, showing it to be within the State; and the treasurer shall thereupon cut off the whole of the ears and of the nose from such skin, and entirely destroy them by burning; then he shall pay the bounty and take the claimant's receipt therefor upon the same paper with such certificate. The town treasurer shall immediately make upon the same paper a certificate under oath, addressed to the Treasurer of State, that he first cut off the ears and nose from the skin of such animal and destroyed them by burning, and then paid said bounty to the claimant.

MOOSE, DEER, AND CARIBOU.

SECT. 9. Whoever hunts, kills, or destroys, with dogs, any moose, forfeits one hundred dollars for every moose so hunted, killed, or destroyed; and no person shall, between the first days of January and October, in any manner hunt, kill, or destroy any moose, under the same penalty.

SECT. 10. Whoever hunts, kills, or destroys, with dogs, any deer or caribou, forfeits forty dollars for every deer or caribou so hunted, killed, or destroyed; and no person shall, between the first days of January and October, in any manner hunt, kill, or destroy any deer or caribou, under the same penalty. Any person may lawfully kill any dog found hunting moose, deer, or caribou. Any person owning or having in possession dogs for the purpose of hunting moose, deer, or caribou, or that are used for such hunting, forfeits not less than twenty nor more than one hundred dollars.

SECT. 11. Whoever has in his possession the carcass or hide of any such animal, or any part thereof, between the first days of January and October, shall be deemed to have hunted and killed the same contrary to law, and be liable to the penalties aforesaid; but he shall not be precluded from producing proof in defense. In case of conviction, such carcass or hide, or any part thereof, so found in his possession, shall be decreed by the court forfeited to the prosecutor. And the warden, or either of his deputies, as named in Section 18, may search for such carcass or hide, or any part thereof, subject to Sections 12, 13, and 14 of Chapter 132; but the warrant may be issued on complaint of said warden or either of his deputies.

NO PERSON ALLOWED TO DESTROY OR HAVE IN POSSESSION MORE THAN ONE MOOSE, TWO CARIBOU, OR THREE DEER.

SECT. 12. Whoever kills, destroys, or has in possession, between the first days of October and January, more than one moose, two caribou, or three deer, forfeits one hundred dollars for every moose, and forty dollars for every caribou or deer killed, destroyed, or in possession in excess of said number; and all such moose, caribou, or deer, or the carcasses or parts thereof, are forfeited to the prosecutor. Whoever has in possession, except alive, more than the aforesaid number of moose, deer, or caribou, or parts thereof, shall be deemed to have killed or destroyed them in violation of law.

TRANSPORTATION FORBIDDEN.

SECT. 13. Whoever carries or transports from place to place the carcass or hide of any such animal, or any part thereof, during the period in which the killing of such animal is prohibited, forfeits forty dollars.

GAME SEIZED MAY BE RETURNED WHEN BOND IS GIVEN.

SECT. 14. Any person, whose game has been seized for violation of the game law, shall have it returned to him on giving to the officer a bond with sufficient sureties, residents of the State, in double the amount of the fine for such violation; conditioned, that if convicted of such violation he will within thirty days thereafter pay such fine and costs. If he neglects or refuses to give such bond and take the game so seized, he shall have no action against the officer for such seizure or for the loss of the game seized.

SHERIFFS, POLICE OFFICERS, AND CONSTABLES CAN ACT AS GAME WARDENS.

SECT. 17. Sheriffs, deputy sheriffs, police officers, and constables are vested with all the powers of game wardens and their deputies, and shall receive for their services the same fees as are prescribed for sheriffs and their deputies for similar services.

MINK, BEAVER, SABLE, OTTER, FISHER, MUSKRAT, AND BIRDS.

SECT. 20. Whoever, between the first day of May and the fifteenth day of October, destroys any mink, beaver, sable, otter, fisher, or muskrat, forfeits ten dollars for each animal so destroyed, to be recovered on complaint.

DUCKS, PARTRIDGES, AND WOODCOCK.

SECT. 21. Whoever kills, or has in his possession, except alive, or exposes for sale, any wood duck, dusky duck, — commonly called black duck,— or other sea duck, between the first days of May and September; or kills, sells, or has in possession, except alive, any ruffed grouse,— commonly called partridge,— or woodcock, between the first days of December and September following; or kills, sells, or has in possession, except alive, any quail or pinnated grouse, — commonly called prairie chicken,— between the first days of January and September, or plover, between the first days of May and August, forfeits not less than five nor more than ten dollars for each bird so killed, had in possession, or exposed for sale. And no person shall kill, expose for sale, or have in possession, except alive, any woodcock or ruffed grouse or partridge during September, October, or November, except for consumption as food within the State, under the same penalty.

SECT. 22. Whoever at any time or in any place, with any trap, net, snare, device, or contrivance other than the usual method of sporting with fire-arms, takes wild duck of any variety, quail, grouse, partridge, or woodcock, forfeits five dollars for each bird so taken. But this section and the preceding do not apply to the shooting of ducks on the sea-coast.

LARKS, ROBINS, SWALLOWS, SPARROWS, AND ORIOLES.
(*R. S., Chapter 30.*)

SECT. 23. Whoever kills or has in his possession, except alive, any birds commonly known as larks, robins, swallows, sparrows, or orioles, or other insectivorous birds, crows and hawks excepted, forfeits not less than one dollar nor more than five dollars for each such bird killed, and the possession by any person of such dead bird is *prima facie* evidence that he killed such bird.

NESTS, EGGS, AND YOUNG BIRDS NOT TO BE DESTROYED.

SECT. 24. Whoever at any time wantonly takes or destroys the nest eggs, or unfledged young of any wild bird, except crows, hawks, and owls, or takes any eggs or young from such nests, except for the purpose of preserving the same as specimens, or of rearing said young alive, forfeits not less than one dollar nor more than ten dollars for each nest, egg, or young so taken or destroyed.

TRANSPORTATION FORBIDDEN.

SECT. 25. Whoever carries or transports from place to place any of the birds named herein, during the period in which the killing of such bird is prohibited, forfeits five dollars for each bird so carried or transported.

PENALTIES.— HOW RECOVERED AND HOW DISPOSED OF.

SECT. 26. All penalties imposed by the six preceding sections may be recovered by action of debt, or by complaint or indictment, in the name of the State, by any warden or his deputies, or any other person in any county in which such offense is committed or the accused resides; and in all actions therefor in the Supreme Judicial or Superior Courts, if the plaintiff prevails, he recovers full costs without regard to the amount recovered. All fines and penalties recovered for violations of the seventeen preceding sections, except Sections 15 and 16, shall be paid, one-half to the complainant and one-half to any game and fish protective society or other sportsmen's association organized under the laws of Maine and located in the county where said fines and penalties are recovered; *provided*, that said society or association expends the same in the propagation and cultivation of trout and salmon for the fresh-water lakes and ponds of the State, under the direction and supervision of the Fish Commissioners. If more than one such society or association is located in such county, said Commissioners shall designate to which society the money shall be paid, or they may cause the same to be divided between them. If there is no such society or association in said county, the Commissioners shall appropriate the same to such society as aforesaid, as they deem proper.

SUNDAY MADE A CLOSE TIME.

SECT. 27. Sunday is a close time, on which it is not lawful to hunt, kill, or destroy game or birds of any kind, under the penalties imposed therefor during other close times; but the penalties already imposed for violation of the Sunday laws are not repealed or diminished.

COMMISSIONERS OF FISHERIES AND COMMISSIONERS OF GAME.

SECT. 28. The powers and duties of the Commissioners of Fisheries and wardens extend to all matters pertaining to game, and they have the same powers to enforce laws pertaining thereto as they have in enforcing the laws relating to the fisheries.

INLAND FISHERIES.

APPLICATION OF THE LAW.

SECT. 29. The following sections apply to all fresh waters above the flow of the tide, and to all tidal waters frequented by the various species of fresh-water and migratory fishes, except to the capture of salmon, shad, and alewives in Denny's River and its tributaries, and Pemmaquam River and its tributaries, and to the taking of white perch in tide waters, or in the stream between Grand Lake on the St. Croix waters and Sysladobsis Lake, known as Dobsis Stream, or within two hundred yards of the head and mouth of said stream, and except as provided in the two following sections.

SECT. 30. This chapter does not apply to that portion of the St. John River and its tributaries lying above Grand Falls in New Brunswick, nor to fish taken in the weirs on St. Croix River; and does not repeal the laws relating to the St. Croix, Denny, Pemmaquam, Cobscook, East Machias, and Narraguagus Rivers; nor does it apply to the taking of blue-back trout; except that no person shall fish for, catch, take, kill, or destroy the same with net, seine, weir, or trap, under a penalty of five dollars for the attempt, and one dollar for each blue-back trout so taken, caught, killed, or destroyed, to be recovered by complaint.

SECT. 31. The following waters and their tributaries are exempt from provisions relating to migratory fishes, and the supervision of fishways by the Commissioners. that is to say; Royall's River in North Yarmouth; Sewall's Pond or its outlet in Arrowsic; Nequasset Stream in Woolwich: so much of the waters of Damariscotta River as are west of the railroad bridge near Damariscotta Mills: Duck Trap Stream in Lincolnville and Belmont; the eastern Penobscot River in Orland; Winslow's and Leach's Streams in Penobscot; all waters in Vinalhaven, Bluehill, Tremont, Mt. Desert, Eden, Franklin, and Sullivan; Tunk River in Steuben; Pleasant River in Washington County; East Machias River and Cobscook or Orange River in Whiting.

DEFINITION OF TERMS.

SECT. 32. For the purpose of the following sections, the term "salmon" means the common migratory salmon of the sea-coast and rivers; the term "land-locked salmon" means any of the species or varieties of salmon that do not periodically and habitually run to the sea, being the same locally known as "salmon trout" and "black-spotted trout"; the term "alewife" means the small species of migratory fish commonly called "alewife," but known also by the local names of "herring" and "gaspereau," and also includes the similar species found in tidal waters and known as "blueback"; and the term "bass" means the striped bass of tidal waters.

COMMISSIONERS OF FISHERIES.

SECT. 33. The Governor, with the advice and consent of Council, shall appoint one or two persons, as they think best, to be Commissioners of Fisheries, who shall hold office for three years, unless sooner removed, and have a general supervision of the fisheries, regulated by the following sections. Commissioners shall examine dams and all other obstructions existing in all rivers and streams, and determine the necessity of fishways and the location, form, and capacity thereof; visit those sections where fisheries regulated by this chapter are carried on, and examine into the working of the laws; introduce and disseminate valuable species of fish into waters where they do not exist, and perform all other duties prescribed by law. They shall report annually on or before the thirty-first day of December to the Governor, who shall cause three thousand copies to be printed. They shall see that violations of the fish laws are duly prosecuted.

FISHWAYS AND DAMS.

SECT. 34. The owner or occupant of every dam or other artificial obstruction in any river or stream naturally frequented by salmon, shad, or alewives, shall provide the same with a durable and efficient fishway, of such form and capacity, and in such location, as may, after notice in writing to one or more of said owners or occupants, and a hearing thereon, be determined by the Commissioners of Fisheries, by written notice to some owner or occupant, specifying the location, form, and capacity of the required fishway, and the time within which it shall be built; and said owner or occupant shall keep said fishway in repair, and open and free from obstruction for the passage of fish during such times as are prescribed by law; *provided*, that in case of disagreement between the Commissioners of Fisheries and the owner or occupant of any dam as to the propriety and safety of the plan submitted to the owner or occupant of such dam for the location and construction of the fishway, such owner or occupant may appeal to the County Commissioners of the county where the dam is located, within twenty days after notice of the determination of the Fishery Commissioners, by giving to the Fishery Commissioners notice in writing of such appeal within that time, stating therein the reasons therefor; and, at the request of the appellant or the Fishery Commissioners, the senior Commissioners in office of any two adjoining counties shall be associated with them, who shall appoint a time to view the premises and hear the parties, and give due notice thereof, and after such hearing they shall decide the question submitted, and cause record to be made thereof, and their decision shall be final as to the plan and location appealed from. If the requirements of the Fishery Commissioners are affirmed, the appellant shall be liable for the costs arising after the appeal, otherwise they shall be paid by the county.

SECT. 35. If a fishway thus required is not completed to the satisfaction of the Fishery Commissioners within the time specified, every owner or occupant forfeits not more than one hundred nor less than twenty dollars for every day of such neglect between the first days of May and November.

SECT. 36. On the completion of a fishway to the satisfaction of said Commissioners, or at any subsequent time, they shall prescribe in writing the time during which the same shall be kept open and free from obstruction to the passage of fish each year, and a copy thereof shall be served on the owner or occupant of the dam. The Commissioners may change the time as they see fit. Unless otherwise provided, fishways shall be kept open and unobstructed from the first day of May to the fifteenth day of July. The penalty for neglecting to comply with this section, or with any regulations made in accordance herewith, is not less than twenty nor more than one hundred dollars for every day of such neglect.

SECT. 37. Whenever the Commissioners find a fishway out of repair or needing alterations, they may, as in case of new fishways, require the owner or occupant to make such repairs or alterations; and all proceedings in such cases, and the penalty for neglect, shall be as provided in the three preceding sections, without appeal.

SECT. 38. If the dam is owned and occupied by more than one person, each is liable for the cost of erecting and maintaining such fishway, in proportion to his interest in the dam; and, if any owner or occupant neglects or refuses to join with the others in erecting or maintaining such fishway, the other owners or occupants shall erect or repair the same, and have an action on the case against such delinquent for his share of the expenses.

SECT. 39. If the owner or occupant of such dam resides out of the State, said penalties may be recovered by a libel against the dam and land on which it stands, filed in the Supreme Judicial Court in the county where it is located, in the name of the Commissioners of Fisheries, or of any fish warden who shall give to such owner or occupant, and all persons interested therein, such notice as the Court, or any justice thereof in vacation, orders; and the Court may render judgment therein against said dam lands for said penalties and costs, and order a sale thereof to satisfy such judgment and costs of sale, subject, however, to all said requirements for the erection and maintenance or repair of said fishway.

FISH WARDENS.

SECT. 40. The Governor, with the advice and consent of Council, may appoint wardens, who shall enforce all laws relating to game and the fisheries, arrest all violators thereof, and prosecute all offenses against the same; they shall have the same power to serve criminal processes against such offenders, and shall be allowed the same fees, as sheriffs for like services: they shall have the same right as sheriffs and their deputies to require aid in executing the duties of their office; and whoever refuses or neglects to render such aid when required forfeits ten dollars, to be recovered upon complaint. Fish wardens shall hold office for three years, unless sooner removed.

PROTECTION OF FISH. — SALMON AND SHAD.

SECT. 41. No salmon, shad, or other migratory fish shall be taken or fished for within five hundred yards of any fishway, dam, or mill-race; nor between the Bangor and Brewer Bridge over the Penobscot River and the water-works dam at Trent's Falls, on said river; nor between the Augusta highway bridge over the Kennebec River and the Augusta dam, between the first days of April and November, except by the ordinary mode of angling, with single hook and line or artificial flies; nor shall hook and line or artificial flies be used at any time within one hundred yards of any fishway, dam, or mill-race. The penalty for violation of this section is a fine of not more than fifty nor less than ten dollars for each offense, and a further fine of ten dollars for each salmon, and one dollar for each shad, so taken.

SECT. 42. From the fifteenth day of July to the first day of April following there shall be a close time for salmon, during which no salmon shall be taken or killed in any manner, under a penalty of not more than fifty nor less than ten dollars, and a further penalty of ten dollars for each salmon so taken or killed: *provided, however*, that between the fifteenth days of July and September it is lawful to fish for and take salmon by the ordinary mode,— with rod and single line,— but not otherwise.

WEEKLY CLOSE TIME.

SECT. 43. Between the first day of April and the fifteenth day of July there shall be a weekly close time of forty-eight hours,—from sunrise on each Saturday morning to sunrise on the following Monday morning,—during which no salmon, shad, alewives, or bass shall be taken. During the weekly close time, all seines, nets, and other movable apparatus shall be removed from the water. Every weir shall have, in that part where the fish are usually taken, an opening three feet wide, extending from the bottom to the top of the weir, and the netting or other material which closes the same while fishing shall be taken out, carried on shore, and there remain during the weekly close time, to the intent that during said close time fish may have a free and unobstructed passage through such weir or other obstruction; and no contrivance which tends to hinder such fish shall be placed in any part thereof. If the enclosure where the fish are taken is furnished with a board floor, an opening extending from the floor to the top of the weir is equivalent to one extending from the bottom to the top. The penalty for the violation of this section is twenty dollars for each offense. This section does not apply to the Kennebec, Androscoggin, or Penobscot Rivers or their tributaries, or to the St. Croix River below the breakwater at the ledge.

LAND-LOCKED SALMON, TROUT, TOGUE, BLACK BASS, AND WHITE PERCH.

SECT. 47. There shall be an annual close time for land-locked salmon,—commonly so called,—trout, togue, black bass, Oswego bass, and white perch, as follows, viz.: For land-locked salmon, trout, and togue, between the first days of October and the following May, except on the St. Croix River and its tributaries and all the waters in Kennebec County, in which the close time is between the fifteenth day of September and the first day of the following May; and for black bass, Oswego bass, and white perch, between the first days of April and July.

SECT. 48. No person shall take, catch, kill, or fish for in any manner, any land-locked salmon, trout, or togue in any of the waters aforesaid between the first days of October and the following May, nor in the St. Croix River and its tributaries between the fifteenth day of September and the first day of the following May, or black bass, Oswego bass, or white perch between the first days of April and July, under a penalty of not less than ten nor more than thirty dollars, and a further fine of one dollar for each fish thus caught, taken, or killed; *provided, however,* that during February, March, and April citizens of the State may fish for and take land-locked salmon, trout, and togue, and convey the same to their own homes, but not otherwise.

SELLING OR TRANSPORTATION OR HAVING IN POSSESSION.

SECT. 49. No person shall sell, expose for sale, or have in possession with intent to sell, or transport from place to place, any land-locked salmon, trout, or togue between the first days of October and the following May, or any black bass, Oswego bass, or white perch between the first days of April and July, under a penalty of not less than ten nor more than fifty dollars for each offense.

SECT. 50. Any person having in possession, except alive, any land-locked salmon, trout, or togue between the first days of October and the following May, or any black bass, Oswego bass, or white perch between the first days of April and July, or who transports from place to place within the State any land-locked salmon, trout, or togue between the first days of October and May following, or black bass, Oswego bass, or white perch between the first days of April and July, shall be deemed to have killed, caught, or transported the same contrary to law, and be liable to the penalties aforesaid.

NETS, SPOONS, SET LINES, AND OTHER FORBIDDEN METHODS.

SECT. 51. Whoever at any time catches, takes, kills, or fishes for any sea salmon or land-locked salmon, trout, togue, black bass, Oswego bass, or white perch by means of grapnel, spear, trawl, weir, net, seine, trap, spoon, set line, or with any device, or in any other way than by the ordinary mode of angling,— with a single-baited hook and line, or with artificial flies,— forfeits not less than ten nor more than thirty dollars for each offense, besides one dollar for each fish so caught, taken, or killed. And all set lines, grapnels, spears, trawls, weirs, nets, seines, traps, spoons, and devices other than fair angling, as aforesaid, are prohibited in all fresh-water lakes, ponds, and streams; and when found in use or operation in said waters they are forfeit and contraband, and any person finding them in use therein may destroy them.

SECT. 52. Whoever fishes for, takes, catches, kills, or destroys any fish, except in tide waters, with net, seine, weir, or trap, forfeits fifty dollars for the offense and ten dollars for each salmon or land-locked salmon so taken, caught, killed, or destroyed.

SECT. 53. Whoever kills or destroys any sea salmon or land-locked salmon less than nine inches in length, or any trout less than five inches in length, forfeits five dollars for the offense, and fifty cents for every sea salmon, land-locked salmon, or trout so killed or destroyed. Whoever has in possession any salmon or trout of less than the above dimensions shall be deemed to have taken them in violation of this section.

NOT OVER FIFTY POUNDS TO BE CAUGHT OR TRANSPORTED.

SECT. 54. No person shall take, catch, kill, or have in possession at any one time, for the purpose of transportation, more than fifty pounds of land-locked salmon or trout, or of both, nor shall any such be transported except in the possession of the owner thereof, under a penalty of fifty dollars for the offense, and five dollars for every pound of land-locked salmon or trout, or both, so taken, caught, killed, in possession, or transportation, in excess of fifty pounds; and all such fish transported in violation of this section may be seized on complaint, and shall be forfeited to the prosecutor. Whoever has in possession more than fifty pounds of such fish shall be deemed to have taken them in violation of this section.

BASS FROM SPAWNING BEDS.

SECT. 55. Whoever takes any black bass during April, May, and June, or at any time, from these spawning beds, forfeits for each offense not more than twenty nor less than five dollars, besides one dollar for each bass so taken.

NETS.

SECT. 56. No net other than a dip-net, the meshes of which are smaller than one inch square in the clear, shall be used in any waters frequented by migratory fishes, except the St. Croix River, between the first days of April and October, under a penalty of not more than twenty nor less than ten dollars for each offense.

INTRODUCTION OF CERTAIN FISH PROHIBITED.

SECT. 57. No muskallonge, pickerel, pike, sunfish or bream, yellow perch, or black bass shall be introduced, by means of live fish or spawn, to any waters where they do not now severally exist, except as hereinafter provided, under a penalty of not more than two hundred nor less than fifty dollars.

SECT. 58. Whoever introduces fish of any kind, except trout, fresh and salt water salmon, fresh-water smelts, blue-back trout and minnows, by means of live fish or otherwise, into any waters now frequented by trout or salmon, except as hereinafter provided, forfeits not less than fifty nor more than five hundred dollars.

Fish Seized may be returned on giving Bond.

Sect. 59. Any person whose fish has been seized for violation of a fish law shall have such returned to him on his giving to the officer a bond with sufficient sureties, residents of the State, in double the amount of the fine for the same; conditioned, that, if the final judgment is guilty, he will, within thirty days thereafter, pay such fine and costs. If he neglects or refuses to give such bond, and to take the fish so seized, he shall have no action against the officer for such seizure or loss thereof.

Sheriffs, Constables, and Police Officers to act as Fish Wardens.

Sect. 66. It shall be the duty of all sheriffs, deputy sheriffs, constables and police officers, as well as fish wardens and their deputies, to cause any person, violating either of the sections from thirty-four to sixty-five inclusive, to be promptly prosecuted, either by complaint, or by giving information to the county attorney. Said officer shall be allowed for said services the same fees as sheriffs and their deputies. They may seize any implement used in illegal fishing, and may render any weir unlawfully built or maintained incapable of taking fish, and may, on view, seize any fish taken or possessed in violation of law.

Fines and Penalties,—how Recovered.

Sect. 67. All fines and penalties named in Sections 35 to 65 inclusive, unless otherwise provided, may be recovered by complaint, indictment, or action of debt; and, in all actions of debt commenced in the Supreme Judicial or Superior Court, the plaintiff prevailing recovers full costs, without regard to the amount recovered. Judges of Municipal and Police Courts, and trial justices, have concurrent jurisdiction of all offenses described in said sections when the penalty does not exceed thirty dollars. Where the offense is alleged to have been committed in any river, stream, pond, or lake forming a boundary between two counties, or where the fish are caught in one county and carried to another, the action, complaint, or indictment may be commenced and prosecuted in either.

Weirs, Hedges, etc.

Sect. 68. No weir, hedge, set-net, or any other contrivance for the capture of fish, which is stationary while in use, shall extend into more than two feet depth of water at ordinary low water, under a penalty of not more than one hundred nor less than fifty dollars, and forfeiture of all apparatus and material so unlawfully used. This provision applies to any sein or drift-net which is at any time attached to a stationary object, but not to fykes or bag-nets used in the winter fishery for smelts and tom-cods, nor to any implements lawfully used above the flow of tide, nor to any portion of the Penobscot River, Bay, or tributaries.

SECT. 69. The limit of depth prescribed for weirs in the preceding section shall be measured at the entrance of the weir; *provided*, that no part of such weir known as the leader is in more than two feet of water at low-water mark. Weirs may exceed the limit of two feet'depth, measured as aforesaid, under the following conditions, namely: first, the distance from the before mentioned two-feet limit to the entrance of such weir shall not exceed one hundred feet; second, no such weir shall obstruct more than one-eighth of the width of the channel; third, every such weir shall be stripped so as to render it incapable of taking fish on and after the twenty-fifth day of June; but these conditions apply only to weirs that exceed the aforesaid limit of depth. The standard for low-water mark on the Kennebec River is in all cases the nearest bench mark of the United States Coast Survey, allowance being made at the various points for the difference in time. The provisions of this and the preceding sections do not apply to fish weirs built on the seashore.

BOATS, IMPLEMENTS, AND MATERIALS USED, AND FISH TAKEN, TO BE FORFEITED.

SECT. 71. All boats, implements, and materials used, and all fish taken in violation of this chapter, are forfeited.

SCRAPS AND OTHER OFFAL.

SECT. 73. Whoever casts or deposits, or causes to be thrown or deposited into any navigable waters, any pomace, scraps, or other offal arising from the making of oil or slivers for bait from menhaden or herring, forfeits not less than fifty nor more than one thousand dollars for each offense, to be recovered by indictment or action of debt in the name and to the use of the county in which the offense is committed; and there shall be a lien on all boats, vessels, crafts, and apparatus of every kind in the possession of any person violating this section, whether owned by him or not; they may be attached in such action, and held to respond to the judgment for the penalties, forfeitures, and costs as in other cases; and any trial justice, on complaint, may cause the arrest of the accused and seizure of the property alleged to be forfeited, and may detain the same until a trial may be had; and on conviction, said property shall be decreed forfeited to the uses aforesaid, to be sold in the same manner as goods taken on execution, and the balance, after deducting fines and costs, shall be paid to the person legally entitled to receive it.

DISPOSITION OF FINES AND PENALTIES.

SECT. 74. All fines and penalties recovered for violations of Sections 30, 41 to 46 inclusive, 48 to 58 inclusive, 61, 63 to 65 inclusive, 68 and 70 shall be paid, half to the prosecutor, and half to any game and fish protective society or other association or associations, or to the Fish Commissioners, as provided in Section 26 of Chapter 30, and under the conditions therein imposed; and all other fines and penalties imposed in this chapter shall be paid, half to the prosecutor and half to the county where the proceedings are commenced and prosecuted.

SPECIAL PROVISIONS NOW IN FORCE ON RANGELEY LAKES AND TRIBUTARIES. SPECIAL LAWS OF 1881, CHAP. 1881.

SECT. 1. No person shall take, catch, fish for, or destroy any trout or land-locked salmon in the Kennebago, Rangeley, Cupsuptic, Mooseluemaguntic, Mollychunkamunk and Welokennebacook Lakes, or in the stream flowing into or connecting said lakes, during the months of February, March, and April of each year.

SECT. 2. No person shall use spawn as bait for fishing in any of the waters named in the foregoing section during the month of September of each year.

SECT. 3. Any person who shall violate the provisions of this act shall forfeit and pay the sum of ten dollars for the attempt, and one dollar for each and every trout and land-locked salmon so taken, caught, killed, or destroyed, to be recovered by complaint before any trial justice, one-half to the complainant and one-half to the town where the complaint is made.

ABBEY &  IMBRIE,

MANUFACTURERS OF

EVERY GRADE OF FISHING TACKLE,

18 VESEY STREET, NEW YORK,

FOURTH DOOR FROM THE ASTOR HOUSE.

Particular Attention given to the Selection of Tackle for the Waters of Maine and Canada.

ANGLERS WILL FIND IT TO THEIR ADVANTAGE TO PURCHASE DIRECT OF THE MANUFACTURERS.

We furnish the best Tackle in the market, at the lowest prices consistent with good work.

UNITED STATES CARTRIDGE CO., Lowell, Mass., U. S. A.,
AMMUNITION MANUFACTURERS.

U. S. CARTRIDGES
are the most reliable in the market. We guarantee satisfaction.
U. S. Improved Copper Primers are the Best.

U. S. WATERPROOF BLACK PAPER SHOT SHELLS
are sure fire, gas tight, have securely fastened head, are made of strong paper that will allow of reloading, and are entirely impervious to water. Order a sample lot of your dealer, and test them.

FOR SALE BY ALL GUN AND HARDWARE DEALERS.

ESTABLISHED 1828.

BOSTON
Fishing Tackle House,

Manufacturers of and Dealers in

FINE FISHING TACKLE
of all kinds.

Rods, Reels, Enamelled Lines, Choice Flies, Etc., Etc.

Jointed Bamboo Rods, our own make and superior finish, eight to twenty-four feet long.

FINE GRADE SPLIT BAMBOO RODS.

We invite special attention to our Extra Quality Split Bamboo Rods, with patent Waterproof Interlocking Ferrules.

DIAMOND WATERPROOF LINES.
Diamond Brand Snelled Hooks and Leaders.

===== BETHBARA, GREENHEART, LANCEWOOD FLY TROUT AND BASS RODS. =====

All kinds of Rods made to order.

FACTORY,
6 FANEUIL HALL SQUARE.

J. S. TROWBRIDGE & CO., 88 Washington St., Boston.

HIND'S BLACK-FLY CREAM,

For Repelling Black-Flies, Mosquitoes, Punkies, and all other Insects,

And protecting the skin from

SUNBURN, IRRITATION, and INFECTION.

Also, invaluable as a remedy for

BURNS, SCALDS, CUTS, BRUISES, &c.

Contains *No Tar*, and leaves *No Stain*, and, being of a semi-solid consistence, is convenient to carry, and no danger of breakage, leaking, or spilling.

PRICE, 25 CTS. PER BOX.   POSTPAID, 28 CTS.

Ladies may use it with perfect confidence, on the most delicate skin.

One of its admirers writes:

"My wife, who frequently accompanies me on my fishing trips, uses it, and finds it a satisfactory remedy for sunburn. We would recommend it heartily. . . . It is so neat and clean, so convenient, *and so effective as a repellant.*" . . .

Sold by dealers in Sporting Goods.

OFFICE OF THE COMMISSIONER OF FISH AND GAME,
DIXFIELD, ME., February 25, 1883.

Mr. A. S. HINDS, Portland:
I have used your "Black-Fly Cream," and have found it a sure preventive against flies and mosquitoes. It is neat and clean. . . . I should not think of going into the woods in flytime without it.
HENRY O. STANLEY.

CYNTHIANA, KY., April 23, 1883.
Please accept my thanks for the "Black-Fly Cream" received. It is the most elegant preparation for the purpose I have seen. . . . Will take great pleasure in recommending it.
Yours very truly,
J. A. HENSHALL.

GLENS FALLS, VT., June 15, 1884.
Mr. A. S. HINDS:
Dear Sir,— I have tried all manner of compounds, but yours is the most thorough, at the same time is cleanly, and not disagreeable.
Yours truly,
A. NELSON CHENEY.

PORTLAND, February 27, 1883.
Mr. A. S. HINDS,
Dear Sir,— I used your "Black-Fly Cream" last season while trout fishing, and found it a perfect success. Was not troubled with mosquitoes while using it. It is the *cleanest* and *best* preparation I ever used.
P. B. BURNHAM.

Prepared by A. S. HINDS, Pharmacist,   -   PORTLAND, MAINE.

WM. R. SCHAEFER & SON,
Manufacturers, Dealers, Agents, and Importers of
Fire Arms, Fishing Tackle, and Sportsmen's Goods,
AT WHOLESALE AND RETAIL.

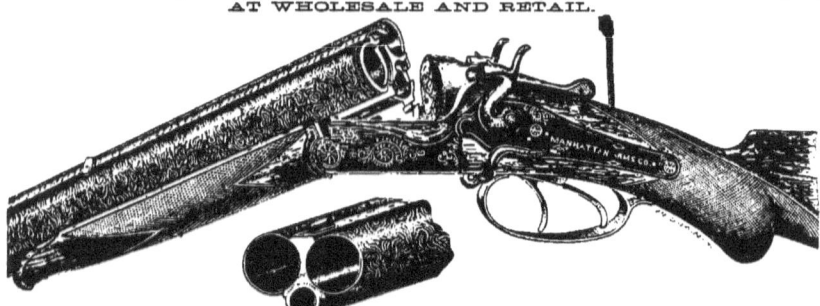

Agents for the celebrated **CHAS. DALY** and **MANHATTAN ARMS CO. THREE BARREL GUNS**, a most effective and desirable weapon for all hunting purposes. It overcomes the necessity of carrying a Shot Gun and Rifle separately. These Three Barrel Guns possess the advantage of having a Double Barrel Shot Gun and Rifle combined in *one*. Can be obtained in all the various gauges and calibres.

ABBEY & IMBRIE'S CELEBRATED FISHING TACKLE.

Send stamp for our new catalogue.   **61 ELM STREET, COR. DOCK SQUARE, BOSTON, MASS.**

Send Five Cents for 80 page Illustrated Catalogue.

FINE GOODS

A SPECIALTY.

OVER THE CARRY.

J. H. RUSHTON, Canton, N. Y.,
BUILDS
PLEASURE BOATS,
HUNTING BOATS, SNEAK BOATS, SAILING AND PADDLING CANOES, CRUISERS,

Steam Launches to order, and has in stock

OARS, ROWLOCKS, SAILS, CLEATS, BLOCKS, ETC., ETC.

MAYNARD RIFLE.

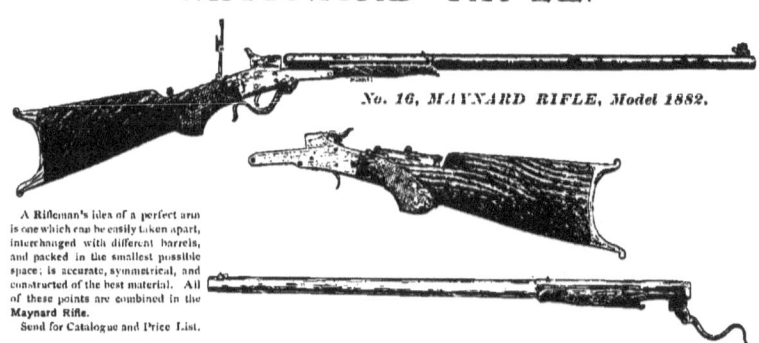

No. 16, MAYNARD RIFLE, Model 1882.

A Riflcman's idea of a perfect arm is one which can be easily taken apart, interchanged with different barrels, and packed in the smallest possible space; is accurate, symmetrical, and constructed of the best material. All of these points are combined in the **Maynard Rifle**.

Send for Catalogue and Price List.

MASSACHUSETTS ARMS COMPANY,
Box 777, CHICOPEE FALLS, MASS.

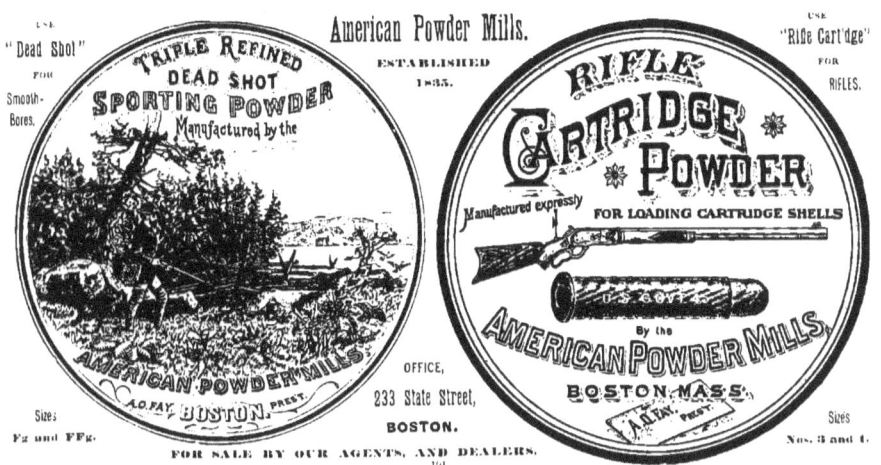

LUCKE & MITCHELL,

SHERBROOKE, P. Q.,

DEALERS IN FISHING TACKLE AND SPORTING GOODS,

desire to call the attention of Sportsmen to their very complete assortment of the above lines.

FLY RODS.

SPLIT BAMBOO FLY RODS, TROLLING RODS, BAIT RODS, &c., &c.

ARTIFICIAL FLIES AND HACKLES.

We have had made to our order a large variety of such FLIES as are best adapted to our lakes and streams.

REELS.

Celluloid, Patent and Brass of all kinds.

LINES.

Enameled Waterproof Silk Lines, Chinese Grass Lines, Braided and Hand Laid Linen Lines.

HOOKS, PHANTOM MINNOWS, CASTING LINES, TROLLING BAITS.

RIFLES, SHOT GUNS, AND REVOLVERS.

A fine assortment of English and American Guns. Colt's, Smith & Wesson, and "Robin Hood" Revolvers. Cartridges and Shells, all sizes.

LUCKE & MITCHELL,

ODELL'S BLOCK,   SHERBROOKE.

THE ONTARIO CANOE COMPANY (Limited),
OF PETERBOROUGH, CANADA,

Gold Medal, London, Eng., Fisheries Exhibition, 1883.

Silver Medal, Montreal, 1884.

Silver Medal, Antwerp, 1885.

Silver and Bronze Medals, Toronto, 1885.

MANUFACTURERS OF

PLEASURE, FISHING, AND HUNTING CANOES,

Patent Cedar Rib, Longitudinal Rib, Basswood, Folding, Decked and Sailing Canoes, Paddles, Oars, Sails, and all Canoe Fittings.

Send Three-Cent Stamp for Catalogue.

J. Z. ROGERS, President.

⇻ JUMBOLENE ⇺

CURES AND PREVENTS
INSECT BITES, SUNBURN, CHAPPED HANDS OR FACE,
OR ROUGHNESS OF THE SKIN,

But does not prevent tanning, and is especially good to protect the hands from blistering while rowing, or from becoming tender and sore while handling fish and fishing tackle.

IT IS THE BEST LINIMENT IN USE
— FOR —

Burns, Scalds, Chilblains, Frost Bites, Sprains, Rheumatic and Neuralgic Pains, &c.

It prevents Blood Poisoning in cuts and other wounds, and promotes rapid healing in all cases.

TRADE-MARK REGISTERED.

SOLD BY DRUGGISTS AND DEALERS IN SPORTING GOODS,
AT 50 CENTS PER BOTTLE.

THOMAS JENNESS & SON, Proprietors,
Bangor, Maine, - - U. S. A.

WHOLESALE AGENTS: Boston — JOHN P. LOVELL'S SONS; New York — VON LENGERKE & DETMOLD, 14 Murray St.

DICKERMAN'S PATENT HAMMERLESS RIFLE,
— WITH —

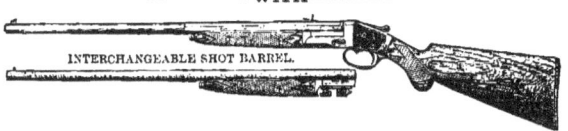

Latest and best combined Sporting Arm. Furnished in leading calibres, from .32 upwards, with suitable Gun Case.

THE DICKERMAN HAMMERLESS SINGLE BARREL SHOT GUN,

Designed especially for Trap-shooting, and furnished with Interchangeable Rifle Barrels of all calibres. 10 and 12 gauges,—three grades,—Damascus, Laminated, and Twist, Close Hard Shooters.

IMPROVED AUXILIARY RIFLE BARREL,
For Breech Loading Shot Guns.

Weight but twenty-eight ounces; all calibres. Indorsed by the *American Field* and *Forest and Stream*, as well as by thousands of Sportsmen. Address, for Circular,

THE STRONG FIRE ARMS CO., - - New Haven, Conn.

HUCKINS' SOUPS.

Green Turtle, Tomato, Mock Turtle, Ox Tail, Chicken, Mullagatawney, Julienne, Okra or Gumbo, Pea, Beef, Consommé, Macaroni, Vermicelli, Soup and Bouilli, Terrapin.

RICH AND PERFECTLY SEASONED. Require only to be heated and are then ready to serve. *Put up in quart cans only.* These soups were first introduced to the public in 1855, and have always maintained their excellence and high reputation. Only the very best material is used in their preparation.

SOLD BY ALL LEADING GROCERS.

J. H. W. HUCKINS & CO.,
Sole Manufacturers, Boston, Mass.

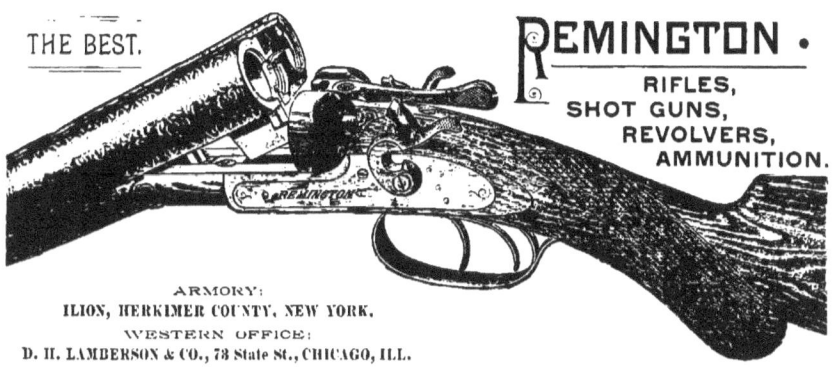

The most convenient item in a Sportsman's outfit is a **Rifle Barrel** always at hand, not an auxiliary affair which is "at home" when wanted, but a Barrel attached to a Shot Gun, which does not to any extent increase the weight, which is positively accurate, which does not alter the beauty and symmetry of the weapon, and in which the blow can be thrown from the Shot to Rifle Barrel instantaneously by a simple device that cannot get out of order. **THE DALY THREE BARREL**, first made in the fall of 1886, is an assured success. The Barrels are fine quality Damascus; the workmanship is as fine as the finest; the shooting remarkable for closeness, evenness, and penetration.

12 gauge, 32 W. C. F., 32-40, 38-55, 40-63, 45-70, 8 to 9 lbs., $85.00.   10 gauge, 38-55, 40-63, 45-70, 8½ to 9½ lbs., $95.00.

SCHOVERLING, DALY & GALES, 84 & 86 Chambers St., New York,

Send for Catalogue of all their Specialties in Guns (just issued).   The **CHARLES DALY HAMMERLESS** is the **Finest Gun in the World.**

MARLIN FIRE ARMS COMPANY,
New Haven, Conn.

SEND FOR ILLUSTRATED CATALOGUE.

MARLIN MAGAZINE RIFLES

Use long cartridges with sufficient powder and lead to do effective work at long range. The flight of the bullet is rapid, and the penetration immense. They are simple and strong, and for accuracy of shooting they excel any other Magazine Rifle in the world.

BALLARD GALLERY RIFLES

are used in most of the large shooting galleries of the country.

BALLARD TARGET RIFLES

are renowned, capturing by far the majority of all the prizes at the shooting tournaments of the country.

Have you seen the New Marlin Double Action Automatic Revolver?

Carte Blanche (Rich.)

Grand Vin Sec (Dry.)

The Highest Grade Champagne in the World.

JOHN D. & M. WILLIAMS, Agents, - 187 State St., Boston, Mass.

The Boston Club Book.

A COMPLETE DIRECTORY OF NAMES AND ADDRESSES OF ALL THE BOSTON CLUBS OF ANY PROMINENCE,

CONTAINING OVER ONE HUNDRED CLUBS, INCLUDING ALL THE BOSTON YACHT, MUSICAL, CLUBS, AND SOCIAL DRAMATIC,

AND OFFICIALLY CORRECT TO DATE.

PRICE, $2.00, BY MAIL, POSTPAID.

EDWARD E. CLARK,

Publisher of the "BOSTON BLUE BOOK,"   41 West Street, Boston, Mass.

For Sale by all Dry and Fancy Goods Dealers.
CALL FOR IT.

SEAVEY, FOSTER & BOWMAN,

NEW YORK,   PHILADELPHIA,
CHICAGO,   BALTIMORE,
ST. LOUIS,   CINCINNATI,
SAN FRANCISCO,   GLOVERSVILLE, N.Y.

BOSTON, MASS., 104 Arch Street.

No Fisherman's Outfit complete without

"REX MAGNUS,"

THE GREAT FOOD PRESERVATIVE.

What a Fisherman says, who tried it.

HUMISTON PRESERVATIVE COMPANY:

Gentlemen,—Being an habitual fisherman, and having caught some fine specimens of trout (on the farm of Charles Parker), one of which weighed over two pounds, I had a desire to preserve them in order to show them to the many callers at my office; and, procuring some "*Viandine*" at your works, I treated three of them, and I am pleased to report that, after exhibiting them in my office for *four weeks*, I then sent them to a friend in Waterbury, where two weeks later I saw the fish and found them still sound and good, with no indications of decay. It is a wonderful thing, and one of the most important in the commissary outfit for sportsman and tourist.

FRED. A. DURANT, Durant's Hotel.

NEW HAVEN, July 1.

Application as simple as that of common salt.

Directions with each package. Sample package of one pound sent by mail on receipt of 50 cents.

THE HUMISTON PRESERVATIVE CO.,

130 Park Street,   NEW HAVEN, CONN., U. S. A.

→ Tobaccos and Cigarettes especially adapted to Sportsmen. ←

STRAIGHT CUT, - SUPERLATIVE, - AND - FRAGRANT VANITY FAIR
—— ✴ CIGARETTES. ✴ ——

FINE SMOKING MIXTURES: THREE KINGS, MELLOW MIXTURE, TURKISH AND VIRGINIA, PERIQUE AND VIRGINIA. SALMAGUNDI. GRANULATED.

—— 14 FIRST PRIZE MEDALS. ——

WM. S. KIMBALL & CO., - Rochester, N.Y.

E. & H. T. Anthony & Co.,
Manufacturers and Importers of
PHOTOGRAPHIC INSTRUMENTS,
APPARATUS and SUPPLIES,
591 BROADWAY, - NEW YORK.

Sole proprietors of the Patent Satchel Detective, Schmid Detective, Fairy, Novel, and Bicycle Cameras, and sole agents for the Celebrated Dallmeyer Lenses. Amateur Outfits in great variety, from $9 upward. Send for Catalogue, or call and examine. ☞ *More than forty years established in this line of business.*

SPORTING OUTFITS.
Flannel Shirts,
Canvas Suits,
Dogskin Jackets,
Helmets, Leggins,
Belts, Knapsacks,
and Canteens.

G. W. SIMMONS & CO.
32 to 44 North St.,
BOSTON.

J. STEVENS ARMS AND TOOL CO.,

P. O. Box 3000, CHICOPEE FALLS, MASS.,

MANUFACTURERS OF THE

Stevens Patent Breech Loading, Sporting, and Hunter's Pet Rifle,

SINGLE AND DOUBLE SHOT GUNS, POCKET RIFLES.

The best scores on record in America, from 10 to 50 yards, have been made with STEVENS PISTOL.

STEVENS GALLERY PISTOLS.

"Conlin" Model, 10 inch barrel, .22 cal., weight, 2 1-8 pounds.
"Lord" Model, 10 inch barrel, .22 cal., weight, 3 pounds.
"Diamond" Model, 10 inch barrel, .22 cal., weight, 11 ounces.
Also, the new 6 inch barrel, .22 cal. Target Pistol.

The new 6 inch barrel Stevens Pistol is carried by those who desire compactness and lightness combined with the greatest accuracy.

STEVENS TARGET PISTOL,

Known throughout the world as possessing unsurpassed accuracy, perfection of form and finish. The professional shots all unhesitatingly select the Stevens Pistols to perform the most difficult feats of marksmanship.

———— Write for our new Price List, as we have made great reductions in prices. ————

Mounted Moose Head For Sale.

(The cut is an exact engraving from a photograph.) Can be seen in the store of Messrs. DAME, STODDARD & KENDALL, 374 Washington St., Boston. Address, H. BISHOP, Hotel Hoffman, Boston, Mass.

· MAP ·

OF THE

Megantic, Spider, and Upper Dead River

REGIONS

(The same as in this book.)

PRINTED UPON PARCHMENT (INDESTRUCTIBLE.)

Folded in a Case to be carried in the Pocket.

For use of Sportsmen while in the Woods.

MAILED, POSTPAID, 25 CENTS.

Address,

H. BISHOP,

Hotel Hoffman, BOSTON, MASS.

OSGOOD'S FOLDING CANVAS BOAT. Weight, for trout fishing, Size of Chest, 36 inches long, with stretcher, side-boards 17 inches wide, 13 inches deep. and paddle, 25 lbs. With stretcher, side-boards, gunwale, stools and oars, 40 lbs. With bottom board, side-boards, gunwale, stools and oars, 50 lbs. This cut shows twelve-foot boat.

THE BEST!
THE SAFEST!
The Lightest! The Steadiest!
The Staunchest and Most Durable!
Impossible to tip it over by Rocking!
Easy to Row! Safest and Best Hunting and Fishing Boat made.
Oars and paddle are jointed, and pack in chest with boat without extra charge.

Makes up four different weights, the same as four boats combined in one.

The above is a view of the Boat in its compact form, showing Boat folded, Bottom-Board, Camp-Stools, Gunwale, Stretcher, and Packing Chest. Oars and Paddles are jointed and packed with Boat in Chest.

AN ILLUSTRATED JOURNAL FOR RIFLEMEN.

This Journal is devoted to the interests of Riflemen throughout the world. Every department of Rifle Shooting is represented in its columns. Practical contributions from experts in the different branches. Profusely and artistically illustrated. Records of tests and experiments. Portraits of the crack Rifle Shots of America. Records of American Riflemen in the various styles of shooting. Published monthly. Subscription price, including postage to any part of the world, $1.50 per annum. **A. C. GOULD & CO., Publishers,**
4 Exchange Place, Boston, Mass.

The · American · Angler.

A Weekly Journal devoted exclusively to Fish, Fishing, and Fish Culture; practical essays on Angling, Anglers' Implements; and reports of fishing from all parts of the United States and Canada. Seth Green, the eminent fish culturist, has charge of the Fish Culture Department. Published weekly, $3.00 per annum. Send for Descriptive Catalogue of Angling Books. **THE ANGLERS' PUBLISHING CO.,**
252 Broadway, New York.

❈ THE PARKER GUN ❈
LEADS THEM ALL IN HARD-HITTING QUALITIES.

Won the best average of five days' shooting at the World's Tournament at Wellington, Mass., May 30 to June 3, 1887; also, the Second Annual Tournament of the Chamberlin Cartridge Co.'s, held at Cleveland, Ohio, September 14, 1886, out of eighty-seven entries from representative shots, representing fourteen States, the **PARKER GUN** won first and third money, winning $900 out of the $1,200 purse offered, adding another victory to 1885, which was the Second International Clay Pigeon Tournament for the championship of the world, held at New Orleans, La., February 11 to 16. Among the contestants shooting other guns were such champions as Carver, Bogardus, Cody, Stubbs, Erb, and others.

PARKER BROTHERS, Makers,
New York Salesroom, 97 Chambers St.   **MERIDEN, CONN.**

Belcher Shot Shell Loader
Makes Loading a Pleasure.

500 AN HOUR, WITH EASE.

Owners of guns cannot afford to be without one. $10 complete for any one gauge. Descriptive circulars sent on application to manufacturer,

CHAS. W. DIMICK,

194 Washington Street,   BOSTON, MASS.

Franklin & Megantic Railroad.

Most Direct and Favorite Route to

DEAD RIVER REGION, BIGELOW LAKES,

AND THE

Celebrated Resorts at Tim, Seven, Spencer, King-Bartlett, and Chain Ponds, in Franklin and Somerset Counties.

ALSO, TO

SPIDER AND MEGANTIC LAKES IN CANADA.

PURE AIR.
    PURE WATER.
        BEAUTIFUL SCENERY.

AND ABUNDANCE OF FISH AND GAME.

Boston to Kingfield in 10 Hours.

All Rail Line, Close Connections.

Purchase Tickets via Maine Central, Sandy River, and Franklin & Megantic Railroads. Early arrivals at terminal points, and excellent Hotel, Livery, Boat, and Guide accommodations.

PHILIP H. STUBBS, Gen. Manager.

◁ BOSTON TO NEW YORK. ▷

SHORE LINE

Leave Providence Railroad Station, Boston, at 10 A. M., 1 and 11 P. M.   Sundays, at 11 P. M.

Leave New York at 8 A. M., 1 and 11 P. M.   Sundays, at 11 P. M.

A. A. FOLSOM, Superintendent.

QUEBEC CENTRAL RAILWAY,

The only short and pleasant route to Quebec from New York, Boston, White Mountains, and all points South and West, via Newport, Vt., and Sherbrooke.

 PALACE DRAWING-ROOM AND SLEEPING CARS ON ALL TRAINS.

The Railway traverses a country full of beautiful lakes and mountain scenery, passes within a few yards of the wonderful Asbestos Mines, and also within a few miles of the great Harvey Hill Copper Mines, and down the

VALLEY OF THE CHAUDIERE RIVER,

immortalized by General Arnold's march on Quebec in 1775, now noted for its celebrated gold mines. Connections are made at Quebec with steamers for the Saguenay River and Lower St. Lawrence, and the Intercolonial Railway for all points in the Maritime Provinces, also with

CANADIAN PACIFIC RAILWAY FOR THE CELEBRATED ST. LEON SPRINGS.

Members of the Megantic Fish and Game Club desiring to take a trip from Sherbrooke to Quebec, the ancient Capital of the Dominion, will be entitled to return tickets at single fare, on presentation of certificates of membership to the Quebec Central Railway Ticket Agent at Sherbrooke. Sportsmen should not fail to avail themselves of this opportunity to visit old Stadacona.

Tickets for sale at W. Raymond's General Ticket Office, 256 Washington Street, Boston; Quebec Central Ticket Office, opposite St. Louis Hotel, Quebec; Union Ticket Office, Sherbrooke, and at all Railroad Ticket Offices.

J. R. WOODWARD, General Manager,
Sherbrooke, Quebec.

J. H. WALSH, Acting Gen'l Frt. & Pass. Agent,
Sherbrooke, Quebec.

"GREEN MOUNTAIN ROUTE."

CENTRAL VERMONT RAILROAD

TO MONTREAL AND ALL POINTS IN CANADA.

J. W. HOBART, Gen'l Manager,　　　J. M. FOSS, Gen'l Supt.,　　　S. W. CUMMINGS, G. P. A.,
ST. ALBANS.　　　　　　　　　　ST. ALBANS.　　　　　　　　　　ST. ALBANS.

I. B. FUTVOYE, Supt. Northern Division, St. Johns, P. Q.

LEADS TO MORE FISHING AND HUNTING RESORTS THAN ANY LINE IN THE COUNTRY.

MAINE CENTRAL RAILROAD.

THE DEAD RIVER REGION.
THE RANGELEY LAKES.
KENNEBAGO AND PARMACHENEE.
MOOSEHEAD LAKE.

AND ALL THE LAKES OF NORTHERN MAINE.

And to the Salmon Waters of the **PENOBSCOT, ST. JOHN, MIRAMICHI, METAPEDIA,** and **RESTIGOUCHE,** as well as the Salmon Streams of Nova Scotia.

Take trains from Boston & Maine R.R. Station in Boston or Worcester, connecting with Maine Central at Portland. Information cheerfully furnished on application to the General Passenger Agent at Portland.

PAYSON TUCKER, General Manager.   **F. E. BOOTHBY, Gen. Pass. Agent.**

CHAMPION
Single Breech Loading Shot Gun.

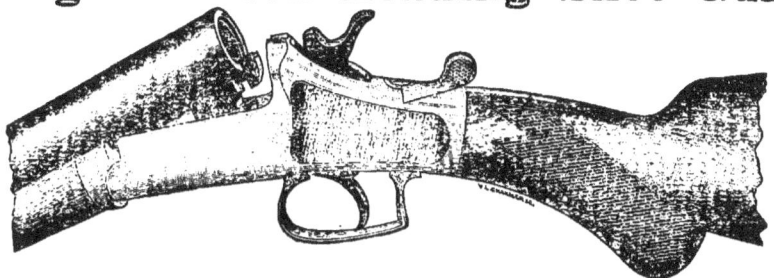

12 Bore, Plain Steel Barrel, ... $15.00		12 Bore, Stub Twist Barrel, ... $18.00
10 " " " " , ... 16.00		10 " " " " , ... 19.00

THE CHAMPION GUN is made either Choke or Cylinder Bore; has Pistol Grip Stock, Rebounding Lock, and Patent Fore End Fastening. As it shoots equally well fine bird shot, duck shot, all sizes buck shot, and round bullets for moose and bear, it is the most effective arm one can secure for use in the woods. Weight only 6 to 8½ lbs. It is rapidly taking the place of the heavy rifle. Send for descriptive catalogue.

JOHN P. LOVELL ARMS CO., 147 Washington St., Boston, Mass.,
Manufacturers, Wholesale and Retail Dealers in
GUNS, RIFLES, REVOLVERS, FISHING TACKLE, AND SPORTING GOODS OF EVERY DESCRIPTION.
Our stock of Fishing Tackle is the finest in the country.
Sole New England Agents for the DOUGLAS FOLDING BOAT, the Best in the World.

★ THE UNITED

Mutual Accident

OF NEW Y

Office, 320 & 322 Broad

P. O. Box

NEW FEA'

$10,000 Death by Accident. $1,3
10,000 Loss of Hands or Feet.   2,5
10,000 Loss of Hand and Foot.
5,000 Loss of Hand or Foot.
5,000 Loss of Both Eyes.

The above combined insu

$26 a year; or, One-Half or One-Qu

Membership Fee, $5 in

———— 37,000 MEM

CHARLES B. PEET,
President.

A WISE OLD DOG.

FREDDIE. "Remember, Prince, it is you and I that go hunting to-day."
PRINCE. "Well, in that case, I think we'd better go and take out a policy in the United States Mutual Accident Association, 320 and 322 Broadway, New York."

www.ingramcontent.com/pod-product-compliance
Lightning Source LLC
Chambersburg PA
CBHW021823230426
43669CB00008B/845